TALK | 1

French

ISABELLE FOURNIER

Series Editor: Alwena Lamping

BBC Active, an imprint of Educational Publishers LLP, part of the Pearson Education Group, Edinburgh Gate, Harlow, Essex CM20 2JE, England

First published 1998
Ninth edition 2017
9

ISBN: 978-1-4066-7890-1

Editor: Geraldine Sweeney
Additional editing: Jenny Gwynne, Tara Alner, Anita Ogier
Project editor: Emma Brown
Insides design: Nicolle Thomas, Rob Lian
Layout: Pantek Media Ltd. www.pantekmedia.co.uk
Illustrations © Mark Duffin
Cover design: Two Associates
Cover photograph: © iStock.com/oksix
Audio producer: John Green, TEFL tapes
Presenters: Marianne Borgo, Stephane Cornicard, Philippe Monnet, Vanessa Seydoux
Sound engineer: Tim Woolf
Studio: Robert Nichol Audio Productions
Music: Peter Hutchings

www.bbcactivelanguages.com

Contents

Introduction

Welcome to the new edition of **Talk French**, the bestselling course from BBC Active which has inspired and helped so many people to learn French from scratch and given them the confidence to have a go.

The key to **Talk French**'s effectiveness is the successful **Talk** method, developed by experienced teachers of languages to adult beginners. Its structured and systematic approach encourages you to make genuine progress and promotes a real sense of achievement. The choice of situations and vocabulary is based on the everyday needs of people travelling to France.

Talk French includes a book and 120 minutes of recordings of French native speakers. The book in this new edition has several additional features, inspired by feedback from users and teachers. There's an extended grammar section (pages 116–128), a two-way glossary (pages 129–144), covering around 1,000 words, and the ever-popular **Talk** *Wordpower* (pages 124–127), designed to increase your vocabulary fast.

There also are links to the **Talk French** video clips and activities on the BBC Languages website at www.bbcactivelanguages.com/FrenchVideoLinks. These cover the contents of this book at the same level but in an alternative way, providing additional exposure and reinforcing the language against the background of French culture. Free tutors' support and activities are available online at www.bbcactivelanguages.com.

How to make the most of Talk French

1   Read the first page of the unit to focus on what you're aiming to learn and set it in context while gaining some relevant vocabulary.

2   Listen to the key phrases – don't be tempted to read them first. Then listen to them again, this time reading them in your book too. Finally, try reading them out loud before listening one more time.

3   Work your way through the activities which follow the key phrases. These highlight key language elements and are carefully designed to develop your listening skills and your understanding of French. You can check your answers at any time in the *Transcripts and answers* starting on page 99.

Wherever you see this: **1•5**, the phrases or dialogues are recorded on the CD (i.e. CD1, track 5).

4 Read the *En français* explanations of how French works as you come to them – this information is placed just where you need it. And if you'd like to know more, visit the relevant pages in the *Grammar* section, indicated by the following symbol: **G13** . For an even deeper level of knowledge, there's a separate **Talk French Grammar** book.

5 After completing the activities, and before you try the *Put it all together* section, listen to the conversations straight through. The more times you listen, the more familiar French will become and the more comfortable you'll become with it. You might also like to read the dialogues at this stage – preferably out loud.

6 Complete the consolidation activities on the *Put it all together* page and check your answers with the *Transcripts and answers*.

7 Use the French you have learnt – the native speaker presenters on the audio will prompt you and guide you through the *Now you're talking!* page as you practise speaking French.

8 Check your progress. First, test your knowledge with the *Quiz*. Then assess whether you can do everything on the checklist – if in doubt, go back and spend some more time on the relevant section.

9 Read the learning hint at the end of the unit, which provides ideas and suggestions on how to use your study time effectively or how to extend your knowledge. Watch the video clip and follow any links that interest you.

10 Finally, relax and listen to the whole unit, understanding what the people are saying in French and taking part in the conversations.

When you've completed the course, go and use your French and enjoy the sense of achievement. If you want to carry on learning, **Talk French 2** is there waiting for you, as is the **Talk French Grammar**, which is so much more than an ordinary grammar book.

Pronunciation guide

French has several sounds that are not used in English, as well as a slightly different rhythm to its sentences, and the only infallible way of acquiring a good French accent is by listening to native speakers and imitating them. However, some preparation is useful before listening: the words in the right-hand columns below are a guide to the sound of the individual letters and combination of letters.

vowels		consonants	
a, à	cat	**c**	**c**ar, **c**lass, **c**od
ai	day	**ce, ci, ç**	**ce**lery, **ci**rcle, si**x**
au	**au**bergine, **o**ver	**ch**	**Ch**ampagne
e	*either* h**e**r *or* g**e**t	**g**	**g**olf, **g**rand
é	caf**é**	**ge, gi**	mira**ge**
è, ê	cafeti**è**re	**gn**	ca**ny**on, Champa**gn**e
ë	No**ë**l	**gu**	ba**gu**ette
eau	gât**eau**	**h**	*almost always silent*
eu	f**u**r	**j**	plea**s**ure
i, î, ï	pol**i**ce	**ll**	*either* vi**ll**age *or* **y**acht
o	h**o**t	**qu**	bou**qu**et, **qu**iche
œ	f**u**r	**r**	*rolled at back of throat*
oi	s**wa**n, cr**oi**ssant	**th**	**t**ear
ou	f**oo**d	**y**	**y**ellow
u, ù	*merged oo and ee*	The other consonants are similar in French and English, although, **b**, **d**, **p** and **t** are softer sounds in French.	
y	pol**i**ce		

A vowel before **n** or **m** has a nasal sound unless there's another vowel after the **n/m** or the **n/m** is doubled: e.g. **vin, pain, faim, bon, cinq, un** are nasal but not **vinaigre, panier, famille, bonne, cinéma, une**. To produce a nasal sound, say the English *sang, song, sung* but stop short before the *ng*. You'll feel the build-up of air in your nostrils.

Wordpower on page 124 has more detail on French sounds.

Bonjour! Ça va?

saying hello and goodbye

asking someone's name

... and introducing yourself

using the numbers 0 to 10

En France ... *In France ...*

greeting people and saying goodbye are often accompanied by a handshake. Close friends and relatives kiss each other on both cheeks – two, three or four times depending on local custom. When greeting someone it is usual to add their name.

When talking to someone you don't know, you address a man as **monsieur** and a woman as **madame**, or **mademoiselle** if she is very young. Followed by a surname, these words are the equivalent of *Mr*, *Mrs* and *Miss* and, in writing, they are usually abbreviated to **M.**, **Mme** and **Mlle**.

Saying hello

1 1•02 Listen to these key phrases.

Bonjour.	Hello./Good morning./Good afternoon.
Bonsoir.	Good evening.
Salut!	Hi!
Ça va?	How are you?
Ça va.	Fine.

Bonjour, madame.

2 1•03 Listen as Christine Picard, the receptionist at the Hôtel Royal, greets people as they pass through the foyer at lunchtime. How many women does she talk to?

3 1•04 It's early evening. Listen to Mme Picard again. Which greeting does she use now?

> **En français ... In French ...**
> Ça va? is a friendly way of asking how someone is or how things are.
> Ça va can be used in a variety of situations to say OK or fine.

4 1•05 Two friends, Marc and Julien, meet in the hotel bar. Listen to the way they greet each other and fill the gaps in their conversation.

Julien	.... **Marc. Ça va?**
Marc	.... **Julien.** ....

5 It's 2 p.m. How would you greet:

- the woman sitting in reception?
- M. Dumas, who you're meeting for the first time?
- Luc, a good friend?

... and goodbye

6   1•06 Listen to these key phrases.

Au revoir.	Goodbye.
Bonsoir.	Goodbye.
Bonne nuit.	Goodnight.
Et ... merci!	And ... thank you!

7   1•07 Christine Picard is now saying goodbye to some guests. Listen and fill the gaps in the conversation.

Christine	**Au revoir, ...**
Monsieur	**.................., madame. Et merci!**
Christine	**Au revoir, ...**
Madame	**Au revoir, madame. ....**

8   1•08 Julien and Marc have been joined by some friends. Listen as Julien says goodnight to some of them and tick any names you hear.

Christine ☐   Danièle ✓   Marc ☐   Pierre ✓

9   Now try the following. How would you:

- say good morning to the Hôtel Royal's waiter?
- ask your friend Michèle how she is?
- say *thank you* to the receptionist as she gives you your key?
- say goodbye to the young woman you have just met in the hotel bar?

> **Au revoir, madame.**

Asking someone's name

1 **1•09** Listen to these key phrases.

Comment vous appelez-vous?	What's your name?
Et vous?	And you?
Enchanté.	Pleased to meet you.
Vous êtes ...?	Are you ...?
Je m'appelle ...	I am called (my name is) ...
Non.	No.
Excusez-moi!	Sorry!

2 **1•10** There's a wedding reception in the hotel. Listen to a conversation between two people and number these phrases as you hear them.

François Suret.	2	**Enchanté.**	5
Comment vous appelez-vous?	1	**Et vous?**	3
Je m'appelle Camille Dupuis.	4		

3 Younger guests at the reception use the informal **Comment tu t'appelles?** to ask *What's your name?* Read their conversation and fill the gaps.

Mélanie	**Comment tu t'appelles?**
Julie	**Julie. Et toi, comment ..tu.. t'appelles?**
Mélanie	**Je ..m'apelle.. Mélanie.**

En français ...

vous and tu both mean *you*. You use:
vous to someone you don't know well and to more than one person
tu to a close friend, a relative or a child
The choice of vous or tu affects other words:

vous	Comment vous appelez-vous?	Et vous?
tu	Comment tu t'appelles?	Et toi?

---

4 **1•11** In the foyer, M. Bruno, the hotel manager, is looking for a Mlle Marty. How many women does he talk to? 2

... and introducing yourself

5   1•12 Listen to these key phrases.

Je suis ...   I am ...
Oui.   Yes.
Enchanté(e).   Pleased to meet you.

En français ...

a man says **Enchanté**, a woman says **Enchantée** – spelt
differently but both sounding the same. Most words which
describe (adjectives) have a masculine and feminine form, with
the feminine (f) usually adding **-e** to the masculine (m).

G4

---

6   1•13 M. Bruno eventually finds Mlle Marty. Listen as he introduces
himself then fill the gaps.

M. Bruno   **Mademoiselle Marty?**
Mlle Marty   **Oui, je ⟨suis⟩ Arlette Marty.**
M. Bruno   **Je ⟨suis⟩ Monsieur Bruno. Enchanté, ⟨Mlle⟩.**
Mlle Marty   ⟨Enchantée⟩ **Monsieur Bruno.**

Using the numbers 0 to 10

1   1•14 Look at the following numbers 0 to 10 and then listen to them
on the audio.

0   1   2   3   4   5   6   7   8   9   10
zéro un deux trois quatre cinq six sept huit neuf dix

2   1•15 Listen and circle the room numbers you hear Christine Picard
calling out to the guests: ③ 4 ⑤ ⑥ 8 ① ⑩

put it all together

1 Match the English with the French.

a	Thank you.	**Ça va?**
b	What's your name?	**Bonsoir!**
c	Are you …?	**Enchanté(e).**
d	I am …	**Je suis …**
e	Good evening!	**Salut!**
f	Pleased to meet you.	**Comment vous appelez-vous?**
g	How are you?	**Merci.**
h	Hi!	**Vous êtes …?**

2 What could these people be saying to each other?

a  　 c

b  　 d

3 Say the following numbers in French, then listen to track 1.14 on the audio to check your pronunciation.

5, 10, 3, 7, 6, 9, 2, 4, 8, 1

4 Can you say the numbers missing from these sequences in French?

- 3, 6, ?
- 0, 5, ?
- 2, 4, ?

now you're **talking!**

1   **1•16** It's mid-morning and you've arrived at a **gîte** near La Rochelle. You ring the bell and the landlady opens the door and greets you.

- **Ah, bonjour, madame!**
- ◆ Ask if she is Mme Tubert.
- **Oui.**
- ◆ Greet her and say who you are.
- **Enchantée.**
- ◆ Say you're pleased to meet her.

2   **1•17** The next day you're on the beach. Mme Tubert's teenage daughter is walking her dog. She greets you.

- **Bonjour, madame!**
- ◆ Say hello and ask her what she's called.
- **Virginie. Et vous?**
- ◆ Say your name.

3   **1•18** That evening, on your way back to your **gîte**, a neighbour greets you.

- **Bonsoir, madame.**
- ◆ Greet him and introduce yourself.
- **Enchanté. Pierre Larrot.**
- ◆ Say you're pleased to meet him.

4   **1•19** A week later, you're leaving.

- ◆ Say goodbye to Mme Tubert and her daughter and thank her.
- **Au revoir ...**

quiz

1 When can you use **Bonjour**?

2 When talking to a child, should you use **vous** or **tu**?

3 What's the French for *Pleased to meet you*?

4 Who would you be greeting if you are using **Salut**?

5 At what time of the day do you say **Bonne nuit**?

6 What do you say to apologise if you have made a mistake?

7 What are the two ways of introducing yourself?

8 When asking a child's name do you ask **Comment tu t'appelles?** or **Comment vous appelez-vous?**

9 What's an informal way of asking how things are going, or saying *OK, fine*?

Now check whether you can ...

- say hello, goodbye and goodnight
- ask someone how they are
- say you're fine
- say thank you
- introduce yourself
- ask someone's name
- apologise if you make a mistake
- use the numbers 0 to 10

Listen to the audio as often as you can and try to imitate the speakers closely. Saying the words and phrases out loud and repeating them many times will help you to become familiar with the sounds of French and make you more confident.

Vous êtes d'où?

giving your nationality

saying where you're from

saying what you do for a living

using the numbers 11 to 20

En France ...

there are 22 **régions** *regions* and 96 **départements** (administrative areas).
Each **département** has a number which makes up the first two figures of
local postcodes.

There are also five overseas French regions: **la Guyane française** *French
Guyana*, and the islands of **Guadeloupe, Martinique, Mayotte** and **la
Réunion**. French is spoken here and is also the mother tongue of people
in parts of **la Belgique** *Belgium*, **le Canada, le Luxembourg** and **la Suisse**
Switzerland. It's widely used in several countries in Africa and is an official
language of the Olympic Movement, the World Health Organisation,
NATO and the UN.

Giving your nationality

1   1•20 Listen to these key phrases.

Vous êtes anglais/anglaise?   Are you English? (m/f)
Je suis américain/américaine.   I'm American. (m/f)
Je suis français/française.   I'm French. (m/f)

En français ...
a final consonant is not normally pronounced. This means that
words like **français** and **anglais** sound slightly different from the
feminine versions, **française** and **anglaise**, with the added **-e**.

---

2   1•21 Read the following statements and decide which were made by
men, and which by women. Listen to the audio to check your answers.

a Je suis français.   b Je suis anglaise.
c Je suis canadien.   d Je suis américain.
e Je suis anglais.   f Je suis australienne.

3   1•22 Match the nationalities to the countries as in the examples, then
listen to some of them on the audio.

anglais(e)   irlandais(e)   américain(e)   écossais(e)
canadien(ne)   français(e)   espagnol(e)

Pays *Country*	Nationalité
l'Allemagne *Germany*	allemand(e)
l'Angleterre *England*	
l'Australie *Australia*	australien(ne)
le Canada *Canada*	
l'Écosse *Scotland*	
l'Espagne *Spain*	
les États-Unis *USA*	
la France *France*	
l'Irlande *Ireland*	
le pays de Galles *Wales*	gallois(e)

Saying where you're from

1 **1•23** Listen to these key phrases.

Vous êtes d'où?	Where are you from?
Vous êtes de ...?	Are you from ...?
Vous êtes de Londres?	Are you from London?
Je suis de ...	I'm from ...

De *from* becomes **d'** before a vowel.

2 **1•24** A group of **étudiants** *students* on a language-learning holiday in Nîmes are asked where they come from by Marie-Pierre, the organiser. Listen and complete their answers.

David	**Je suis de** .... , **en** ....
Anita	**Je suis de** .... , **en** ....
Paul	**Je suis de** .... , **en** ....

En français ...

the word for *in* with most countries is **en** because countries are usually feminine:

en France, en Angleterre, en Australie

... but for masculine countries it is **au** and for plural **aux**:

au Canada	*in Canada*
au pays de Galles	*in Wales*
aux États-Unis	*in the USA*

---

3 **1•25** The students are then encouraged to ask questions in French. Listen as Paul asks Marie-Pierre and M. Michaud where they come from and tick the right answer.

Marie-Pierre	Bordeaux ▢	Bayeux ▢
M. Michaud	Nantes ▢	Nîmes ▢

4 How would you tell a French person where you come from?

Saying what you do for a living

1 **1•26** Listen to these key phrases.

Quelle est votre profession?	What do you do for a living?
Je suis professeur.	I'm a teacher.
... infirmier/infirmière.	... a nurse. (m/f)
... retraité(e).	... retired. (m/f)
Je ne suis pas ...	I'm not ...
Je ne travaille pas.	I don't work.

2 **1•27** Listen to three people in the group being asked about their work and decide which one is an architect, which one a secretary and which one an engineer. Note that *a/an* is not used in French when saying your job title.

> **architecte**
> **secrétaire**
> **ingénieur**

a ....
b ....
c ....

En français ...

to say that you don't do something, you put the words **ne** and **pas** before and after what you don't do.

Je <u>ne</u> travaille <u>pas</u>.	*I don't work.*
Je <u>ne</u> comprends <u>pas</u>.	*I don't understand.* **G7**

---

3 **1•28** Of the other three people asked, two don't work and one doesn't understand the question. Listen and fill the gaps in the conversation.

Marie-Pierre	**Paul, quelle est votre profession?**
Paul	**Je ne travaille pas. Je suis ....**
Marie-Pierre	**Et vous, quelle est votre profession?**
David	**Je suis ....**
Marie-Pierre	**Et vous, Marianne, vous êtes ....?**
Marianne	**Excusez-moi, je ne .... pas.**

Using the numbers 11 to 20

1   **1•29** Listen to the following numbers, then practise saying them.

11 **onze**	12 **douze**	13 **treize**	14 **quatorze**
15 **quinze**	16 **seize**	17 **dix-sept**	18 **dix-huit**
19 **dix-neuf**	20 **vingt**		

2   Write in the numbers missing from these sequences:

a   **six, dix, ..., dix-huit**
b   **onze, ..., treize**
c   **treize, seize, ...**
d   **huit, douze, ..., vingt**
e   **douze, ..., dix-huit**

3   **1•30** Listen to some numbers being read out in random order and underline the ones you hear:

16   11   19   13   20   15   12   14

Which one was not mentioned? What is it in French?

4   **1•31** Now listen as Marie-Pierre gives the numbers of some French **départements** and write them down under the name.

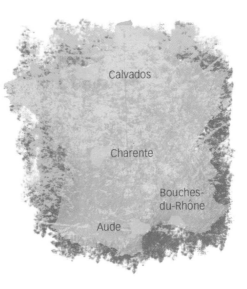

Calvados

Charente

Bouches-du-Rhône

Aude

a   Calvados   14

b   Charente   16

c   Aude   11

d   Bouches-du-Rhône
   13

put it all together

1 Read this conversation between Marie-Pierre and Barbara and fill the gaps with words from the box.

Marie-Pierre	**Vous êtes** ....?
Barbara	**Non, non. Je suis** ....**.**
Marie-Pierre	**Ah, vous** .... **anglaise!**
	Et vous êtes de Londres?
Barbara	**Non, je** .... **de**
	Chichester.

> anglaise
>
> suis
>
> êtes
>
> française

2 How would the following people say where they are from and what their nationality is?

Example: Lina: Madrid, Spain

Je suis de Madrid, en Espagne. Je suis espagnole.

a Rosie: Sydney, Australia
b Celia: Manchester, England
c Andrew: Glasgow, Scotland
d Philippe: Nice, France
e Jane: Los Angeles, United States
f Catherine: Toronto, Canada

3 Can you say these results in French?

| France 12 | Ireland 15 | Wales 11 | England 14 |
| Canada 17 | USA 16 | Australia 20 | Germany 19 |

4 Complete the following in words and figures:

a **quinze + quatre =** .... b **onze + neuf =** ....

c **seize - trois =** .... d **douze + deux =** ....

now you're talking!

1 **1•32** While in Toulouse, a young woman asks you where **la gare** *the station* is.

- ● **Excusez-moi, monsieur. La gare, s'il vous plaît?**
- ◆ Say you're not from Toulouse.
- ● **Vous n'êtes pas français?**
- ◆ Say no, you're English.
- ● **Vous êtes d'où?**
- ◆ Say you're from Birmingham. Ask her where she's from.
- ● **Je suis de Séville.**
- ◆ You haven't understood. What do you say?
- ● **Je suis de Séville. Je suis espagnole.**

2 **1•33** On holiday in France you get chatting to a woman. Answer her questions with information about yourself.

- ● **Bonjour, madame. Vous êtes américaine?**

- ● **Vous êtes d'où?**

- ● **Comment vous appelez-vous?**

3 **1•34** A French man you have just met asks you about your work.

- ● **Quelle est votre profession?**
- ◆ Say you are an engineer. Ask him what he does.
- ● **Je suis professeur.**

quiz

1 How would you tell someone in French that you're from Bristol?

2 Would a man or a woman say **Je suis française**?

3 What two words would you add to this sentence to say you don't work? **Je .... travaille ....**.

4 Would you say **Je suis infirmière** if you are a teacher?

5 How many is **quinze**?

6 What do the first two figures in a French postcode represent?

7 What would you say to let someone know you don't understand?

8 Which is the odd one out? **Américain**, **Espagne**, **France**

9 What's the female version of **italien, égyptien, marocain**?

10 What's the male equivalent of the female professions: **avocate** *lawyer*, **caissière** *cashier* and **pharmacienne** *pharmacist*?

Now check whether you can ...

- say what nationality you are
- say where you're from
- say what your occupation is
- ask others for the above information
- say you don't understand
- use the numbers 11 to 20

It's a good idea at this stage to start organising your vocabulary learning. When learning new words, write them out. Whether it's on paper, your phone, a computer or tablet, the actual process of reproducing them helps to fix them in your memory. Make your vocabulary bank relevant to you and your lifestyle – it's easier to remember words that are important to you.

Voici Émilie

introducing friends and family
saying how old you are
talking about your family

En France ...

la famille *the family* is valued, family responsibilities are taken seriously and people like to talk about their children. Don't be surprised to be asked about your family and don't be reserved about asking questions yourself.

In recent years there have been fewer marriages and an increase in the number of one-parent families. An unmarried partner is introduced as **mon ami** (m) or **mon amie** (f).

Introducing friends

1   1•35 Listen to these key phrases.

Voici Émilie.	This is/Here is Émilie.
... mon mari.	... my husband.
... ma femme.	... my wife.
Voici mes amis.	Here are my friends.

2   1•36 Isabelle Ferri is staying at a campsite near Roscoff. Listen as some neighbours introduce themselves to her and tick the names you hear.

Julien ☐   **Émilie** ✓   **Patrick** ☐   **Marion** ☐   **Nicolas** ✓   **Benoît** ☐

What is Julien's wife called? *Marion*

En français ...

there are three words for *my*:

mon for masculine words or before a vowel

mon mari	*my husband*
mon amie	*my girlfriend/my partner*

ma for feminine words

ma femme	*my wife*

mes for more than one

mes amis	*my friends*

---

3   1•37 Isabelle's husband arrives. Listen and tick:

- what his name is   **Benjamin** ✓   **Luc** ☐
- what nationality he is   **canadien** ✓   **espagnol** ☐

4   1•38 Later, by the pool, the Ferris listen to people chatting. Are Catherine and Bernard single, married, divorced or widowed?

	célibataire *single*	marié(e) *married*	divorcé(e) *divorced*	veuf/veuve *widowed*
Catherine				
Bernard				

... and family

5   1•39 Listen to these key phrases.

Vous avez des enfants?	Do you have any children?
J'ai ...	I have ...
... une fille.	... one/a daughter.
... un fils.	... one/a son.
Je n'ai pas d'enfants.	I don't have any children.

En français ...

un means both *one* and *a/an*. It changes to une for the feminine:

<u>un</u> fils, <u>une</u> fille

des can mean *some* or *any*:

Vous avez des enfants?	*Have you any children?*
Il a des enfants.	*He has (some) children.*

But to say *not any*, you use de/d':

Je n'ai pas d'enfants.	*I don't have any children.*

G3

---

6   1•40 Listen and note how many children Isabelle, Émilie and Marion have.

	fils	fille
Isabelle		
Émilie		
Marion		

7   Near them on the campsite is a proud **grand-mère** *grandmother*. Read what she says to Isabelle – **a** means *has*.

Isabelle	**Vous avez des enfants?**
Grand-mère	**Oui, j'ai une fille, Sabine, et un fils, Luc.**
	Sabine a un fils, Jean-Claude. Luc n'a pas d'enfants.

Can you say what her daughter's name is, whether she has a son and how many grandchildren she has?

Saying how old you are

1 1•41 Listen to these key phrases.

Vous avez quel âge?	How old are you?
Tu as quel âge?	How old are you?
J'ai 20 ans.	I am 20.

2 1•42 Listen and repeat some of the following numbers.

21	**vingt-et-un**	40	**quarante**
22	**vingt-deux**	41	**quarante-et-un**
23	**vingt-trois**	42	**quarante-deux**, etc.
24	**vingt-quatre**	50	**cinquante**
25	**vingt-cinq**	51	**cinquante-et-un**
26	**vingt-six**	52	**cinquante-deux**, etc.
27	**vingt-sept**	60	**soixante**
28	**vingt-huit**	61	**soixante-et-un**
29	**vingt-neuf**	62	**soixante-deux**, etc.
30	**trente**		note that **et** is only used to link 20,
31	**trente-et-un**		30, 40, 50 and 60 with **un**
32	**trente-deux**, etc.		

3 1•43 Listen and underline any of the following numbers you hear:

25   27   31   33   40   42   51   58   61   67

4 1•44 At the seaside, Isabelle hears some young people chatting. Listen and note down their ages.

Aurélien ....   *Alex* ....   *Élisabeth* ....

5 1•45 M. and Mme Blanc are asked their ages when they enrol for a scuba diving course. Listen and tick the right boxes.

	40	41	45	50	51	55
Mme Blanc						
M. Blanc						

Talking about your family

1   **1•46** Listen to these key phrases.

Il/Elle s'appelle comment?	What is his/her name?
Il/Elle s'appelle ...	He/She's called ...
Il/Elle a quel âge?	How old is he/she?
Il/Elle a huit ans.	He/She is eight.

En français ...

to talk about age, you use **avoir** *to have*.
Il a huit ans *He's eight* literally means *He has eight years*.
Avoir changes depending whether it is with **je**, **tu**, **il/elle**, or **vous**:

j'**ai** *I have*	il/elle **a** *he/she has*
tu **as** *you have*	vous **avez** *you have*

G9

---

2   **1•47** Isabelle now asks a neighbour at the campsite about her children. Fill the gaps with the words in the box. Then check with the audio.

Isabelle	**Vous** .... **des enfants?**
Marie-Charlotte	**Oui, j'ai une** ....
Isabelle	**Elle s'appelle comment?**
Marie-Charlotte	.... **s'appelle Valérie.**
Isabelle	**Elle a quel** .... ?
Marie-Charlotte	**Elle** .... **vingt-et-un** ....

> a
> avez
> âge
> fille
> elle
> ans

3   **1•48** Listen to Alain, Catherine and Sabine talking about their families and decide which family belongs to whom.

a ....   b ....   c ....

put it all together

1

Philippe Dorier = Chantal
(père) | **(mère)**

Julie   Antony   **Benjamin** = Laura
(sœur) **(frère)**

Élodie (13 ans)

Look at Benjamin's family tree and underline the correct
ending for his statements. Can you guess what **est** means?

a **Ma mère s'appelle**   **Philippe, Chantal, Laura**

b **Antony est**   **mon frère, mon fils, mon père**

c **Ma fille a**   **trois ans, treize ans, trente ans**

d **Julie est**   **ma femme, ma mère, ma sœur**

e **Mon père s'appelle**   **Antony, Philippe, Benjamin**

f **Laura est**   **ma fille, ma femme, ma mère**

2 Complete the following statements with **ai**, **as**, **a** or **avez**.

a **Ma fille** .... **huit ans.**

b **Vous** .... **un fils?**

c **J'** .... **deux enfants.**

d **Tu** .... **quel âge?**

e **Je n'** .... **pas de sœurs.**

3 Look at Martine's family tree and
fill the gaps in the following text.

Martine = Marc

Benoît   Delphine
(23 ans)   (21 ans)

Je .... **Martine.**
Mon .... **s'appelle Marc.**
J'ai un .... **et une** ....
Mon fils a .... **ans. Il s'appelle** ....
Ma fille a .... **Elle** .... **Delphine.**

now you're talking!

1 **1•49** Answer the following questions as if you are Sophie Smith, married to Michael, with two children, Anna (12) and Martin (14).

- **Bonjour, madame. Comment vous appelez-vous?**

- **Vous êtes mariée?**
- *Introduce your husband.*

- **Vous avez des enfants?**

- **Et votre fille, elle s'appelle comment?**

- **Elle a quel âge?**

- **Et votre fils, il s'appelle comment?**

- **Il a quel âge?**

2 **1•50** You've now started chatting to a woman sitting next to you by the pool.

- Ask her if she's married.
- **Je suis divorcée.**
- Ask her if she has any children.
- **Oui, j'ai un fils, Théo.**
- Ask her how old Théo is.
- **Il a quatorze ans. Ah, voici Théo!**
- Say hello to Théo and introduce Martin and Anna to him.

quiz

1 If you have a daughter, do you have **un fils** or **une fille**?
2 Would you use **mon** or **ma** with **mari**?
3 What is the French for *single*?
4 How would you say that you don't have any children?
5 When referring to your sister's age, would you say **Il a ... ans** or **Elle a ... ans**?
6 To ask a small child how old he or she is, would you say **Tu as quel âge?** or **Vous avez quel âge?**
7 Can you say how old you are in French?
8 If **Henri a cinquante ans**, is he 5, 15 or 50?

Now check whether you can ...

- introduce someone – male or female
- say whether you are married or otherwise
- say what family you have
- give your age
- ask others for the above information
- ask or say how old someone else is
- use the numbers 21 to 69

Family photographs provide ideal practice of the language you have learnt in this unit. Point to people and say who they are and what their name is, e.g. **Voici mon fils. Il s'appelle Paul**. You can say how old some of them are – **Louise a 19 ans** – or what they do – **elle est étudiante**. The following words might come in useful:

cousin/cousine	*cousin* (m/f)
beau-père, belle-mère	*father-in-law/stepfather, mother-in-law/ stepmother*
beau-frère, belle-sœur	*brother-in-law, sister-in-law*

Un thé, s'il vous plaît

ordering a drink in a café

offering, accepting or refusing a drink

asking the price of drinks

En France ...

to order food and drinks in a café, don't queue at the bar as you would in a pub in the UK, but choose a table and wait to be served.

If the waiter/waitress is a bit slow in coming, you can get his/her attention by saying: **Monsieur, s'il vous plaît!** or **Madame, s'il vous plaît!**

Prices in cafés vary a lot depending on the popularity of the place. You'll also pay more if you sit outside.

Ordering a drink

1 1•51 Listen to these key phrases.

Vous désirez?	What would you like?
Un thé, s'il vous plaît.	A tea, please.
... au lait	... with milk
... au citron	... with lemon
Pour moi, un café.	For me, a coffee.
Voilà!	Here you are!
Très bien.	Very well.
alors	then, well then/Right!

2 1•52 Listen to Pierre and Nathalie ordering teas in a café. Do they order tea with milk or with lemon, or do they order **thé nature** (black tea)?

Nathalie   ....Lait..................

Pierre   ......Citron........

En français ...

all nouns (not just those referring to people) are either masculine or feminine and this affects the words for *a* and *the*.
The words for *a* are **un** (m) and **une** (f).

un café ✓	*a coffee*	un jus de fruits	*a fruit juice*
un vin rouge	*a red wine*	un jus d'orange ✓	*an orange juice*
un vin blanc	*a white wine*	un coca	*a coke*
une limonade	*a lemonade*	une pression	*a draught beer*
une bière ✓	*a beer*	une eau minérale	*a mineral water*

G1, G3

---

3 1•53 Four friends join Pierre and Nathalie. Listen to the drinks being ordered and tick the ones you hear on the list above.

... in a café

4 **1•54** Jean, the waiter, is confirming some drinks orders. Has he got them right? Listen out for **bouteilles** *bottles*.

a **un coca, une limonade, un Orangina**
b **un café, une pression et deux Schweppes**
c **deux bouteilles de champagne**
d **un vin blanc et une eau minérale**

En français ...

as in English, nouns usually add **-s** when there are more than one but in French you don't hear it:

>   **Une bouteille de champagne, s'il vous plaît.**
>   **Deux bouteilles de champagne, s'il vous plaît.**   **G2**

---

5 **1•55** Listen to Pierre and Nathalie ordering coffees for their friends. Refer to the **En France ...** box below and fill the gaps.

Jean	**Vous .... ?**
Nathalie	**Deux cafés, un .... café et un .... crème.**
Jean	**Alors deux .... , un .... et un .... crème.**

En France ...

coffee is very strong and therefore served in small quantities. If you order **un café**, you'll get an expresso. If you want a bigger coffee, ask for **un grand café** *a large coffee*. If you want a white coffee, ask for **un café au lait** or **un café crème**.

Offering, accepting or refusing a drink

1 **1•56** Listen to these key phrases.

Qu'est-ce que vous désirez?	What would you like?
Vous voulez un apéritif?	Do you want an aperitif?
D'accord.	OK./Agreed.
Oui, merci.	Yes, please.
Non, merci.	No, thank you.
À votre santé!	Cheers!

2 **1•57** Michel is offering his new neighbours, M. and Mme Blois, an aperitif. Mme Blois only wants **un verre d'eau** *a glass of water*. Listen and fill the gaps below.

Michel	**Vous .... un apéritif, Madame Blois?**
Mme Blois	**Non, merci. Pour ...., un verre d'eau.**
Michel	**Et vous, Monsieur Blois? Un apéritif?**
M. Blois	**Oui, ...**
Michel	**Qu'est-ce que vous ....? Un martini, un porto, un whisky?**
M. Blois	**Un porto, s'il vous plaît.**
Michel	**D'accord. .... À votre santé!**

À votre santé!

Can you guess what **un porto** is?

En français ...
there are various ways of asking the same question. To ask *What would you like?* you can either use Qu'est-ce que ...? *What ...?*:

> **Qu'est-ce que vous désirez?**

or simply make the statement Vous désirez sound like a question by raising your intonation at the end.

> **Vous désirez?**

G5

Asking the price of drinks

1 **1•58** Listen to these key phrases.

C'est combien?	How much is it?
Ça fait ...	That'll be ...
un euro, soixante-dix	1 euro, 70 centimes

2 **1•59** Listen to some of these numbers between 70 and 100.

70	**soixante-dix**	80	**quatre-vingts**
71	**soixante-et-onze**	81	**quatre-vingt-un**
72	**soixante-douze**	82	**quatre-vingt-deux**, etc.
73	**soixante-treize**	90	**quatre-vingt-dix**
74	**soixante-quatorze**	91	**quatre-vingt-onze**
75	**soixante-quinze**	92	**quatre-vingt-douze**
76	**soixante-seize**	93	**quatre-vingt-treize**
77	**soixante-dix-sept**	94	**quatre-vingt-quatorze**, etc.
78	**soixante-dix-huit**	99	**quatre-vingt-dix-neuf**
79	**soixante-dix-neuf**	100	**cent**

3 **1•60** Now listen as Pierre and Nathalie check prices in their local bar. Tick the price you hear.

une bouteille de vin	13,80 €	13,85 € ✓	13,90 €
un verre de champagne	7,70 € ✓	7,75 €	7,77 €
deux martinis	9,24 €	9,48 €	9,80 € ✓

4 **1•61** Jean is adding up three orders. Listen and write down the totals.

a 10.80   b 12.90   c 11.75

En France ...

the currency is the **euro**, written as **€**. There are 100 **cents** or **centimes** in one **euro**. 10,50 € = **dix euros, cinquante (cents)**; 100 € = **cent euros**; 200 € = **deux cents euros**.

put it all together

1   You want to order the following drinks. Would you use **un** or **une**? Fill the gaps.

a .... café   b .... bière   c .... thé

d .... limonade   e .... coca   f .... Orangina

g .... eau minérale   h .... jus de fruits

2   Match up the questions and answers:

a	Qu'est-ce que vous désirez?	Une limonade, s'il vous plaît.
b	C'est combien?	Oui, un jus d'orange.
c	Vous désirez un thé au lait?	Ça fait douze euros.
d	Vous voulez un jus de fruits?	Non, un thé au citron.
e	Vous voulez un apéritif?	Oui, un martini, s'il vous plaît.

3   Complete this conversation with the words from the box:

Jean	**Vous** ....?
Nathalie	**Un thé,** ....
Jean	**Nature, lait,** ....?
Nathalie	**Au lait.**
Jean	...................!
Nathalie	**C'est** ....?
Jean	**Un euro, soixante.**
Nathalie	**Voilà.** ....

> Voilà
>
> Merci
>
> combien
>
> désirez
>
> citron
>
> s'il vous plaît

4   Complete the following:

a   **quarante-cinq + sept =** ....

b   **soixante et onze + neuf =** ....

c   **cinquante-trois + vingt =** ....

d   **quatre-vingt-quinze - cinq =** ....

now you're talking!

1   **1•62** Imagine you're sitting in a café in Nantes.

  ◆ Call the waiter over.
  ● **Bonjour, messieurs dames. Vous désirez?**
  ◆ Order one large coffee, a tea and an orange juice.
  ● **Très bien. Merci.**
  ◆ When the drinks arrive, thank the waiter and ask how much it comes to.
  ● **Ça fait 5,20 €.**
  ◆ Give him the money and say *Here you are*.

2   **1•63** Now imagine you're having a drink in a smart café in Paris. The waitress greets you.

  ● **Madame, monsieur, bonjour. Vous désirez?**
  ◆ Order a coke and a beer.
  ● **Bouteille? Pression?**
  ◆ Order a draught beer.
  ● **Très bien.**
  ◆ When the drinks arrive, ask the price.
  ● **Ça fait 10,70 €.**

3   **1•64** It's your birthday. **Joyeux anniversaire!** *Happy birthday!* How would you order a bottle of champagne?

4   **1•65** Your French neighbours on the campsite have come for a chat.

  ◆ Ask them if they want an aperitif.
  ● **Oui, merci.**
  ◆ Ask them what they'd like. A martini or a whisky?
  ● **Pour moi, un martini.**
  ● **Un whisky pour moi, s'il vous plaît.**
  ◆ Give them their drinks and say *Cheers!*

quiz

1 Which is the odd one out: **eau**, **champagne**, **vin**, **bière**?
2 Do you order **un grand café** or **un café crème** if you want a white coffee?
3 Name three drinks beginning with **c** in French.
4 Is **quatre-vingt-dix** 70 or 90?
5 If you want draught beer do you ask for **bouteille** or **pression**?
6 How do you say *Cheers!* in French?
7 Which is the most expensive part of a café to drink in?
8 What does **C'est combien?** mean?
9 How would you accept if someone offered you a drink?
10 If **pour** means *for*, how would you say *an orange juice for my son* in French?

Now check whether you can ...

- order a drink in a bar
- offer someone a drink
- accept when someone offers you a drink
  ... or refuse politely
- say *Cheers!*
- ask the price of drinks
- understand and use the numbers 70 to 100

Make your French learning relevant to *you* and part of your everyday life. When you have a drink, think of the word in French; when buying a round of drinks, try to memorise the list in French. If you have a dictionary, you can increase your vocabulary by looking up any drinks you, your friends and family enjoy.

Contrôle 1

1   Choose the right phrase for each situation.

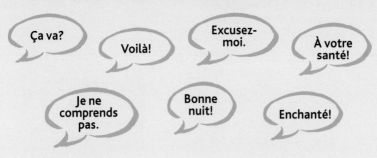

Ça va?

Voilà!

Excusez-moi.

À votre santé!

Je ne comprends pas.

Bonne nuit!

Enchanté!

a   saying *Cheers!*
b   you're off to bed
c   handing someone a drink
d   you don't understand
e   you're introduced to someone
f   you want to apologise
g   you ask someone how they are

2   **1•66** Listen to Mme Chevalier checking in at the hotel and complete her details on the form below. Note how French people give their phone numbers two digits at a time.

Nom:	CHEVALIER
Prénom:	
Adresse:	avenue de la Gare
	30100 Alès
Numéro de téléphone:	04 98 35

Can you say your home, work and mobile phone numbers in French?

3   **1•67** Listen to students from the Nîmes language school
   introducing themselves. Choose the right nationality from the list
   and complete the table. Also, correct any mistakes that have crept
   into the table.

anglais	**anglaise**
allemand	**allemande**
espagnol	**espagnole**
canadien	**canadienne**

Nom	Nationalité	Domicile *Home*
Rosanna		**Barcelone**
Wilfried		**Munich**
Élisabeth		**Stirling, Écosse**
Nicole		**New York**
Paul		**Londres**

4   **1•68** Listen as Jean, the waiter, reads out some prices from the
   menu. Number the prices you hear in the order you hear them.

14,50 €	7,30 €	8,75 €	20,45 €	17,75 €	6,90 €
....	....	....	....	....	....

5   **1•69** Practise
   pronouncing the
   names of these French
   towns, then check your
   pronunciation with the
   audio. Note that **h** is
   silent in French and that
   the final **s** is not spoken
   in any of these names,
   as with most French
   words ending in **s**.

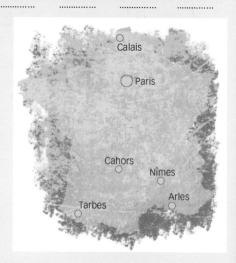

6   1•70 Imagine you're in a French café. The waiter comes over.

- **Bonjour, ... Vous désirez?**
- ◆ Order one white tea, one beer and one glass of water.
- **Très bien ... la bière: pression ou bouteille?**
- ◆ Ask for a bottle.

The waiter brings the drinks and says:

- **Vous êtes américain(e)?**
- ◆ Say no, English.
- **Vous êtes d'où?**
- ◆ Say you are from Bristol.

- ◆ Later on, ask how much it is.
- **Ça fait 10,70 €.**
- ◆ Give the money and say thank you.

7   Draw your family tree with parents, brothers and sisters and your children if you have any. Imagine you are introducing each member to a French acquaintance. Can you say who they are and how old they are?

8   A neighbour asks for your help when her daughter receives a letter in French from a Swiss penfriend. Translate the first page of the letter for them. Some extra vocabulary is given on the right.

Chère Anna,
Je m'appelle Julie. Je suis de Genève, en Suisse. J'ai 14 ans.

J'ai un frère et une sœur. Ma sœur a 18 ans, elle est fille au pair en Allemagne. Mon frère a 23 ans. Il est en France. Il est marié mais il n'a pas d'enfants.

Mon père est architecte et ma mère est professeur de français.

cher/chère	*dear*
Suisse	*Switzerland*
professeur de français	*French teacher*

9   Can you find six drinks in this **mots cachés** *word puzzle*?

C	A	F	E	C	R	E	M	E	B	E
J	U	S	D	E	F	R	U	I	T	S
Z	X	V	B	C	O	C	A	F	H	P
S	D	M	L	P	W	T	Y	X	E	V
X	M	L	O	P	Q	R	P	X	H	E
V	I	N	R	O	U	G	E	M	V	T
O	R	N	B	V	X	P	B	K	Z	S
B	I	E	R	E	G	H	J	T	A	X

Learning a new language often involves guessing the meaning of words. Many French and English words have the same root, so you can guess with confidence. However, remember that while words may look the same or similar, they generally sound quite different – you've already met some of these – **six**, **orange**, **fruits**, **architecte** and **Irlande**.

Où est la poste?

asking where something is

... and how far it is

saying where you live and work

En France ...

most towns have bypasses. If you're driving and wish to visit the centre of a town, look out for the sign **CENTRE-VILLE**. Otherwise follow the sign **TOUTES DIRECTIONS** *all directions*.

The railway station (**la gare**) is often indicated by the abbreviation **SNCF**.

If you need to declare the loss or theft of any belongings, go to the police station (called **gendarmerie** in the country and **commissariat** in a town) or the **mairie** *town hall*.

Asking where something is

1 **1•71** Listen to these key phrases.

Pardon …	Excuse me …
Où est la poste?	Where is the post office?
Où sont les magasins?	Where are the shops?
C'est ici/là.	It's here/there.
Le cinéma est en face de la gare.	The cinema is opposite the station.
La gare est près de l'église.	The station is near the church.

2 **1•72** Pierre asks Virginie to point out some local landmarks on his map. First check the meanings of the words in the glossary.

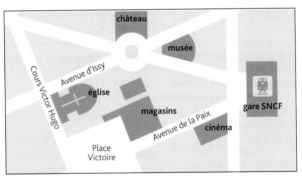

Now listen and match the buildings with the phrases below.

a .... **c'est ici**   b .... **est en face de la gare**

c .... **est là**   d .... **sont près de l'église**

En français …

the words for *the* are:

le	m	le château, le magasin
la	f	la banque *bank*, la poste
les	plural m/f	les magasins, les églises

le and la become **l'** before a vowel or h: **l'hôtel, l'église**   G3

... and how far it is

3 **1•73** Listen to these key phrases.

C'est loin?	Is it far?
C'est à dix minutes.	It's ten minutes away.
C'est à cent mètres.	It's a hundred metres away.
C'est à cinq cents mètres	It's five hundred metres
... de la gare.	... from the station.

4 **1•74** Listen to some tourists enquiring how far **la plage** *the beach*, **le marché** *the market* and the town centre are. Note down what they're told.

	la plage	le marché	le centre-ville
distance			

5 **1•75** Now listen as they enquire about some other places and fill the gaps.

a .... est à côté du café.
b .... est avant la gare.
c .... est en face de l'église.
d .... est après le château.
e C'est à trois .... mètres de la banque.

> **à côté de** *next to*
> **avant** *before*
> **après** *after*
> **en face de** *opposite*

En français ...

de and le combine and become du:
en face du château
à côté du café

G3

Saying where you live

1 **1•76** Listen to these key phrases.

Vous habitez où?	Where do you live?
J'habite ...	I live ...
Il/Elle habite ...	He/She lives ...
... en ville.	... in town.
... à la campagne.	... in the countryside.
... dans un petit village.	... in a small village.

2 **1•77** Bernard asks three people he has just met where they live. Listen and tick the right box.

	en ville	à la campagne	dans un petit village
1			
2			
3			

3 **1•78** Later, one of his colleagues asks him where he lives, using the informal **tu habites**. Listen to discover whether he lives in town or not.

En français ...

the ending of a verb e.g. **habiter** *to live*, **travailler** *to work*, changes if it is with **je, tu, il/elle, nous** *we*, **vous** or **ils/elles** *they*.

		travailler	habiter
I	je/j'	travaill<u>e</u>	habit<u>e</u>
you	tu	travaill<u>es</u>	habit<u>es</u>
he/she	il/elle	travaill<u>e</u>	habit<u>e</u>
we	nous	travaill<u>ons</u>	habit<u>ons</u>
you	vous	travaill<u>ez</u>	habit<u>ez</u>
they	ils/elles	travaill<u>ent</u>	habit<u>ent</u>

All except the **nous** and **vous** forms sound exactly the same. A large group of French verbs end in **-er** and follow this pattern. **G5**

... and work

4 1•79 Listen to these key phrases.

Vous travaillez où?	Where do you work?
Je travaille ... à Paris.	I work ... in Paris.
Il/Elle travaille ...	He/She works ...
... dans un bureau.	... in an office.
... chez Peugeot.	... at Peugeot.
... chez moi.	... at home.
... pour une compagnie américaine.	... for an American company.

5 1•80 Listen to Bernard talking about himself and his family and finish the sentences with one of the key phrases.

Mon frère travaille ....
Ma sœur travaille .... **Elle travaille** ....
.... **Et ma femme travaille** ....
Moi, je travaille chez moi.

Where does Bernard work?

> **En français ...**
>
> chez X means *at the house/home/place/company of X*.
> **Chez mon frère.** *At my brother's house.*

6 1•81 Now listen to some people who do not work. Tick the reason why.

	mère de famille *housewife*	au chômage *unemployed*	retraité(e) *retired*	étudiant(e) *student*
a				
b				
c				
d				

put it **all together**

1 If you were looking for the places listed
   below which signs would you follow?

   a station
   b museum
   c castle
   d market

   MUSÉE

   CHÂTEAU

   GARE SNCF

   MARCHÉ

   MAIRIE

2 The grid below shows the distance between a few northern
   towns and Dunkerque. Practise reading them aloud. For
   example, **Calais est à quarante-deux kilomètres**.

Calais	Lille	Boulogne	Le Touquet	Montreuil
42 km	77 km	80 km	95 km	98 km

3 Do you know the correct form of *the* to use – **le**, **la**, **l'** or **les**
   for each of these places?

   a .... **musée**   b .... **hôtel**
   c .... **gare**   d .... **restaurant**
   e .... **cinéma**   f .... **poste**

4 Read these statements and say whether they are **vrai** *true* or
   faux *false* for you and your town.

   a **La banque est en face de la poste.**
   b **Le musée est à côté de l'église.**
   c **J'habite près du cinéma.**
   d **Je travaille dans un bureau à cent mètres de la gare.**

now you're talking!

1 1•82 Imagine you're in the **office du tourisme** *tourist office* and the clerk is showing you the map of the town.

- ◆ Ask him where the hotel is.
- ● **C'est là.**
- ◆ Now ask where the castle is.
- ● **Le château, c'est là, en face de la mairie.**
- ◆ Ask if it's far.
- ● **Non, c'est à cinq minutes d'ici** *from here.*
- ◆ Ask where the museum and the church are.
- ● **Alors, le musée est ici et l'église est là.**

2 1•83 It's the afternoon and you're now in a café.

- ◆ Call the waitress and order a white coffee.
- ● **Bien, Madame.**
- ◆ Ask her where the bank is.
- ● **C'est là, à cent mètres du café.**

Later on you start chatting to her.

- ◆ Ask her if she lives in town.
- ● **Non, j'habite dans un petit village à la campagne.**
- ◆ Ask if it's far.
- ● **Non, c'est à vingt kilomètres.**

3 1•84 Now she asks you a few questions. Can you tell her:

- ◆ what nationality you are?
- ◆ where you are from?
- ◆ where you live – town, countryside or small village?
- ◆ what your job is?
- ◆ where you work?

quiz

1 What do **le** and **la** both mean?

2 If someone works **dans un bureau**, where do they work?

3 **Avant** is the opposite of ....

4 Does **à côté de** mean *next to* or *opposite*?

5 If you're looking for the station, do you ask for **la gare** or **la poste**?

6 If **cinq cents mètres** is 500 metres then what do you think the French for 400 metres would be?

7 How would you say *It's 10 minutes away* in French?

8 Is the French for *shop*: **château**, **magasin** or **musée**?

9 How do you say that London is 75 kilometres away?

Now check whether you can ...

- ask where a specific place in town is
- ask if it's far
- understand basic town signs
- ask others where they live and work
- give this information about yourself

Learning the patterns of French (i.e. the grammar) allows you to say what you want to say without relying on set phrases.

Parler is the French for *speak* and it follows exactly the same pattern as **habiter** and **travailler**. So, to say what languages you speak, you say for example **Je parle anglais, je ne parle pas allemand**. To ask if someone speaks English, you say **Vous parlez anglais?** (The French words for languages are the same as the masculine nationalities on page 16.)

Il y a une piscine ici?

asking for a specific place

... and making simple enquiries

understanding basic directions

... and asking for help to understand

En France ...

when you're reading a French road map, bear in mind that **A** indicates an **autoroute** or motorway; **N** indicates a **route nationale** or main road which is usually very busy; **D** a **route départementale** or small road – normally very pleasant to drive on as long as you're not in too much of a hurry!

Most motorways are signposted in blue and are toll roads (**autoroutes à péage**). If you drive a long distance, you'll have to pay several times because sections of motorway belong to different companies. You can pay by credit card.

Asking for a specific place

1   2•01 Listen to these key phrases.

Il y a une piscine ici.	There is a swimming pool here.
Il y a des magasins.	There are some shops.
Il y a un supermarché ici?	Is there a supermarket here?
Il y en a trois.	There are three.
Il n'y a pas de … ici.	There aren't any … here.

En français …

il y a means *there is* and *there are*. You add **en** *of them* when specifying a number:

> Il y **en** a deux. *There are two of them.*

There is not/*There are not* is Il n'y a pas de …

> Il n'y a pas de restaurants ici.

---

2   2•02 Listen to people enquiring about local amenities in Boulogne. Some you have already met, some you will be able to guess or look up in the glossary. Link each one with its location.

a	**des taxis**	**rue de la Gare**
b	**un supermarché**	**place du Marché**
c	**une piscine**	**centre-ville**
d	**des magasins**	**place de la République**
e	**un camping**	**centre-ville**
f	**un parking**	**rue de Paris**

la rue *street*
la place *square*

3   How would you ask if there is one of the following?

- campsite
- post office
- swimming pool
- bank

... and making simple enquiries

4   **2•03** Listen to the key phrase.

Est-ce qu'il y a ...	Is there ...
... un garage	... a garage
... près d'ici?	... near here?

En français ...

Est-ce que ...? is a phrase which you will often hear tacked on to the beginning of a question. It doesn't change the meaning at all.

> **Est-ce qu'il y a un garage?/Il y a un garage?**
> *Is there a garage?*

G6

---

5   **2•04** Caroline's **voiture** *car* has broken down. Listen to the audio and read the dialogue below. Then find the French for ...

a   *my car has broken down*
b   *a phone box*
c   *over there*

Caroline	**Excusez-moi, monsieur. Ma voiture est en panne. Est-ce qu'il y a un garage près d'ici?**
Monsieur	**À douze kilomètres, madame.**
Caroline	**Oh, c'est loin! Il y a une cabine téléphonique près d'ici?**
Monsieur	**Oui, il y en a une là-bas.**

6   **2•05** Now listen to four tourists making enquiries. Is the map correct? Change it if necessary.

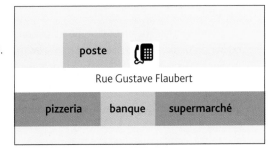

Understanding basic directions

1   **2•06** Listen to these key phrases.

Pour aller à ...?	How do I get to ...?
Allez tout droit.	Go straight on.
Continuez tout droit.	Carry straight on.
Tournez à droite.	Turn right.
Tournez à gauche.	Turn left.
Prenez ...	Take ...
... la première à droite	... the first on the right
puis ...	then ...
... la deuxième à gauche.	... the second on the left.

2   **2•07** Listen to Caroline making some more enquiries. Which letters on the map correspond to the following three places?

- **l'office du tourisme**

- **le marché**

- **l'hôpital** *hospital*

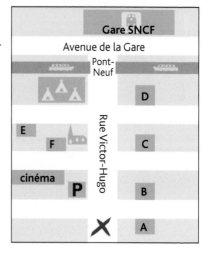

En français ...

you'll notice that the ordinal numbers (*second*, *third*, *fourth*, etc.) all end in -**ième** – **deuxième**, **troisième**, **quatrième**, etc. The one important exception is *first*, which is **premier/première** (m/f).

3   **2•08** Caroline now enquires about the station, the cinema and the campsite. Listen and look carefully at the map above. Are these three places correctly marked on the map?

... and asking for help to understand

4   **2•09** Listen to these key phrases.

Vous pouvez ...	Can you ...
... répéter, s'il vous plaît?	... repeat, please?
... parler plus lentement?	... speak more slowly?

5   **2•10** Two English tourists find it difficult to understand the directions they are given. Can you help them? Listen to the audio and note down which way they should be going.

Peter ....

Anna ....

6   **2•11** Peter is now looking for a swimming pool. Listen and fill the gaps in the dialogue below.

Peter	**Il y a une .... ici?**
Dame	**Oui, place de la République. Prenez la .... à droite, puis tournez à ....**
Peter	**Vous pouvez .... , s'il vous plaît?**
Dame	**Oui, ... la deuxième à droite, puis tournez à gauche. C'est .... de la République.**
Peter	**Merci, Madame.**

7   **2•12** Anna isn't sure how to get back to the station to catch her train home. Listen and note down the route she should take.

....

8   How would you ask:

- if there's a bank near here?
- if there's a campsite near the station?
- someone to repeat what they said?

put it all together

1   Complete each gap in the text with one
    word from the box.

    - .... aller à l'Hôtel du Golf, s'il
      vous plaît?
    - Continuez tout ...., ...
      à gauche puis prenez la ....
      à droite, juste en .... de la
      poste.
    - Vous pouvez parler plus ....,
      s'il vous plaît?

    > pour
    > face
    > deuxième
    > lentement
    > droit
    > tournez

2   You are now looking for the swimming pool. A passer-by
    gives you some directions.

    **La piscine? Allez tout droit, prenez la troisième à gauche
    et c'est à droite, après le camping.**

    Now look again at the map on page 54 and see if you can
    mark the position of the swimming pool.

3   Using **il y a** and **il n'y a pas de**, can you say what there is
    and what there isn't in your home town?

4   Can you make the connection? Match a word from each
    column.

a	piscine	autoroute
b	gauche	banque
c	hôpital	eau
d	panne	infirmière
e	euro	droite
f	à péage	garage

now you're **talking!**

1   **2•13** Imagine you are in Villeneuve for the first time and need some help to find your way around.

♦ Stop a female passer-by politely and ask if there's a tourist office here.

● **Prenez la deuxième à droite et puis la première à gauche.**

♦ Ask whether it's far.

● **Non, c'est à dix minutes.**

♦ Ask whether there's a post office nearby.

● **Oui, il y en a une après la place du Marché, à gauche.**

♦ You didn't quite catch the last bit – ask her to repeat that.

● **La poste est après la place du Marché, à gauche.**

♦ Thank her and say goodbye.

2   **2•14** You've now found the tourist office.

♦ Ask the man behind the desk if there's a bank near here.

● **Il y en a trois. Il y en a une place du Marché.**

♦ You don't understand. Ask him to speak more slowly.

● **Il y a une banque place du Marché. Continuez tout droit et prenez la deuxième rue à gauche.**

♦ Ask him if it's far.

● **Oh, non, c'est à cinq minutes.**

♦ Ask him if there's a cinema here.

● **Non, il n'y a pas de cinéma ici.**

♦ Thank him and say goodbye.

3   **2•15** Later, you're walking in the town centre when another tourist stops you for directions.

● **Pardon. Il y a une banque près d'ici?**

♦ Say the bank is over there, on the right.

● **Là-bas, à droite? C'est loin?**

♦ Say, no, it's two minutes away.

quiz

1 How do you say *there is* or *there are*?
2 Where do you go if your car is **en panne**?
3 What does the sign **péage** on the motorway mean?
4 If you want a quiet drive should you choose a **route départementale** or a **route nationale**?
5 Fill the gap: **première**, ..., **troisième**.
6 If you want a swim do you look for the sign **place, parc** or **piscine?**
7 What word do you need to add to **Il y** .... **a trois** to mean *There are three of them*?
8 True or false? **Vous pouvez parler plus lentement?** means *Could you repeat that, please?*
9 How would you tell someone there isn't a market?

Now check whether you can ...

● ask if there is a specific place in town
● make simple enquiries
● ask how to get to a specific place
● understand basic directions
● ask someone to repeat something or talk slowly
● say *first*, *second*, etc. in French

The best way to make progress is to speak French as often as you can. Keep it very simple and don't worry about mistakes at this stage – you will learn more by practising than by waiting until you're word perfect. Don't hesitate to ask people to repeat what they have said or to speak more slowly.

Je voudrais une chambre

saying which type of room you want

... and how long you want it for

booking a room and paying for it

En France ...

you'll find that hotels are often cheaper than their British equivalents. They charge per room rather than per person, but breakfast is usually extra. If you see the sign COMPLET, it means the hotel is full.

You won't often find bed and breakfasts in towns, but when driving through the countryside you'll see them indicated by the occasional CHAMBRES D'HÔTES sign.

Hotels and campsites are usually well signposted, but don't be misled by the signs HÔTEL DE VILLE, which indicates the town hall and not a hotel, and HÔTEL DES IMPÔTS, which is a tax office.

Saying which type of room you want

1 **2•16** Listen to these key phrases.

Je voudrais une chambre ...	I would like a room ...
... pour une personne	... for one person
... pour deux personnes	... for two people
au premier (1ᵉʳ) étage	on the first floor
avec ...	with ...
... salle de bains.	... bathroom.
... douche.	... shower.
... WC.	... toilet.

2 **2•17** Listen to Nicolas enquiring about a single room in the Hôtel Royal. Does he choose one with a shower or a bathroom?

3 **2•18** As Nicolas waits in reception he listens to someone asking for a double room. Does he want it ...

a **avec deux lits?**

b **avec un grand lit?**

4 **2•19** Listen to two more people choosing their rooms. Tick the floor they choose.

	1ᵉʳ étage	2ᵉ étage	3ᵉ étage	4ᵉ étage
a				
b				

(**deuxième**, **troisième**, etc. are often abbreviated to **2ᵉ**, **3ᵉ**, etc.)

5 How would you ask for these rooms?

●   ●   ●

... and how long you want it for

6 **2•20** Listen to these key phrases.

Pour combien de nuits?	For how many nights?
Pour ...	For ...
... une nuit.	... one night.
... trois nuits.	... three nights.
... une semaine.	... one week.
... ce soir.	... tonight.
... demain.	... tomorrow.

7 **2•21** The Hôtel Royal is busy. Listen to four people asking about a room and note down how long they wish to stay. Listen out for **seulement**, which means *only*.

a ....

b ....

c ....

d ....

8 **2•22** If you book into a hotel in France the receptionist may ask you to spell your name – **Vous pouvez épeler?** Listen to the alphabet in French and make sure you know how to spell out your name.

A B C D E F G H I J K L M N O P Q R S T U V W X Y Z

9 **2•23** Listen to more of Nicolas's conversation with the receptionist. His **prénom** *first name* is Nicolas – can you work out what his **nom** *surname* is?

10 Now practise spelling the names of your friends and relations.

Booking a room

1 **2•24** Listen to these key phrases.

Je voudrais réserver une chambre ...	I'd like to book a room ...
... pour le premier septembre.	... for September 1st.
... du 2 au 5 mai.	... from 2nd until 5th May.

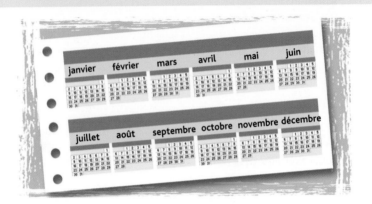

En français ...

for dates, you use **premier** for the first of the month and cardinal numbers (**deux, trois, quatre,** etc.) for the other days.

le premier juillet	*the first of July*
le quatorze avril	*the fourteenth of April*

2   **2•25** Listen to four people talking about their bookings and note down their dates.

a   **Pour** ....

b   **du** .... **au** .... **juin**

c   **Pour** ....

d   **du** .... **au** .... **août**

3   Now it's your turn. Say you'd like to book a room – **Je voudrais réserver une chambre** – for the following dates:

a 15/7   b 10/4   c 1/8   d 3–6/9   e 11–14/5   f 1–4/6

... and paying for it

4   2•26 Listen to these key phrases.

Le petit déjeuner est compris?	Is breakfast included?
Non, il est en supplément.	No, it's extra.
Je peux payer ...	Can I pay ...
... avec une carte de crédit?	... by credit card?

5   2•27 Listen to Marie enquiring about rooms in the Hôtel Royal. Do they cost **cent quinze euros**, **cent cinquante euros** or **deux cents euros**? Tick the right price.

Price of rooms   **115 €**   **150 €**   **200 €**

En français ...

cent *hundred* adds an **-s** only when the number is in round hundreds:

     deux-cents *200*, **cinq-cents** *500*

but ...

     deux-cent-cinquante *250*, **cinq-cent-un** *501*

---

6   2•27 Now listen to the last conversation again. Will the hotel accept payment by credit card? How much extra is breakfast **par personne** *per person*?

Petit déjeuner   **7 €**   **8 €**   **18 €**

7   How would you:
- say you'd like to book a double room with bath for a week?
- ask how much it is?
- ask if breakfast is included?
- ask if you can pay by credit card?

put it all together

1 Find the right ending for the following:

a Je voudrais une chambre pour ...	premier étage
b Je voudrais une chambre avec ...	semaine
c C'est pour une ...	en supplément
d Je peux payer avec ...?	deux personnes
e Le petit déjeuner est ...?	épeler, s'il vous plaît
f C'est huit euros ...	compris
g La chambre est au ...	deux lits
h Vous pouvez ...?	une carte de crédit

2 Now how would you ask ...

a for a double room for a week?
b for a single room for three nights?
c if breakfast is included?
d for a room on the second floor?

3 If you asked the proprietors of the Hôtel du Château the following questions, would they answer **oui** or **non**?

a Le petit déjeuner est en supplément?
b Il y a un parking?
c C'est loin, le centre-ville?
d Il y a une piscine?

Hôtel du Château
Alvignac, Tél. 05.65.33.60.14

- 35 chambres avec s.d.b., TV
- Prix des chambres: 70/80 €
- Petit déjeuner: 9 €
- Parking privé
- À 500 m du centre-ville

now you're talking!

1　**2•28** Imagine you're driving down to Cannes with a friend and you need to find a room for tonight. You've found a hotel you like the look of.

◆ Greet the male receptionist and say you'd like a room for tonight.
● **Oui, madame. Qu'est-ce que vous désirez?**
◆ Say you'd like a double room.
● **Très bien. Avec un grand lit ou avec deux lits?**
◆ Say you'd like a room with twin beds.
● **Bien. Avec salle de bains ou avec douche?**
◆ Say with bathroom, and ask how much it is.
● **Une chambre pour deux personnes avec salle de bains, ça fait 60 €.**
◆ Ask whether breakfast is included.
● **Non, il est en supplément.**
◆ Ask how much it is.
● **Ça fait 6,50 € par personne.**

2　**2•29** You enjoyed your stay so much that you decide to use the hotel for your return trip.

◆ Say you'd like to book a room for 22nd July. This time you'd like a room with twin beds and a shower.
● **Oui, madame.**
◆ Ask if you can pay by credit card.
● **Oui, madame.**
◆ Ask how much it is.
● **Ça fait 53 €, madame.**

quiz

1 Would you be able to get breakfast at an **hôtel de ville**?

2 When do hotels put up the sign **complet**?

3 If you want a shower in your room do you ask for a **salle de bains** or a **douche**?

4 If your room is on the fourth floor, is it **au cinquième étage** or **au quatrième étage**?

5 Name three months which begin with **j** in French.

6 How do you spell in French the name **Dupuis**?

7 True or false: you could go for a swim before breakfast if the hotel has a **piscine**?

8 Is a week **un soir**, **une nuit** or **une semaine**?

9 Fill the gaps to say that the room is for my daughter: **La** .... **est** .... **ma** ....

10 What's the French for *there's no water*?

Now check whether you can ...

- ask for a single or double room
- specify what kind of double room you want
- say what washing facilities you want
- say how long you wish to stay
- understand which floor your room is on
- say you'd like to book a room
- spell out your name

Before you listen to, or take part in, a conversation, picture yourself in that particular situation. What would you say and hear if you were in a hotel in your own country, for example? This helps you to anticipate the language that will be used in French and makes it easier to understand what you hear.

Contrôle 2

1   **2•30** You've heard about a local **propriété** (house where you can buy wine). You ask for directions. Listen and fill the gaps in English:

Take the .... direction; just after Saint-Pey-d'Armens
take the .... on the .... After 5 km, turn ....
At the village of Saint-Sulpice turn .... Carry on for
.... metres. The house is on the right .... the river.

2   **2•31** Listen to Camille Degrave being interviewed for her local radio station and tick the correct details below.

a   She lives   in town ☐
                in the countryside ☐
                in a small village ☐

b   She lives   next to the post office ☐
                next to the station ☐
                opposite the church ☐

c   She works   in a shop ☐
                in an office ☐
                in a bank ☐

d   She is   a dentist ☐
             a secretary ☐
             an architect ☐

e   She is   35 ☐
             45 ☐
             55 ☐

3   **2•32** Camille's company regularly receives visitors from its head office. Listen as her colleague tells Camille when to expect them and note down the dates.

M. Rolland, du .... **au** ....
M. Boulanger, du .... **au** ....
Mme Aubert, du .... **au** ....
Mlle Michaud, du .... **au** ....

4   **2•33** Nicolas is now staying in a little village in Provence. How far away are the following towns? Listen and circle the right distance.

a   **Avignon**   60 km, 62 km, 72 km
b   **Marseille**   45 km, 85 km, 95 km
c   **Cannes**   43 km, 83 km, 93 km
d   **St-Tropez**   78 km, 88 km, 98 km

5   **2•34** Listen to four people booking hotel rooms, and note the details in the boxes.

	no. of people		
a	☐	☐	☐
b	☐	☐	☐
c	☐	☐	☐
d	☐	☐	☐

6   Read these questions and answers and choose a word from the box to fill the gap in each sentence.

parles
habite
travaille
travaillez
parle
habitez

a   **Vous .... dans un magasin?**
    Non, je .... chez moi.
b   **Tu .... anglais? Oui, et je ....**
    aussi allemand et français.
c   **Vous .... ici? Oui, j' .... en ville.**

7   Which sign would you follow if …

a   your car has broken down?
b   you want a list of campsites in the area?
c   you want a room for the night?
d   you want to go swimming?
e   you want to attend a religious service?
f   you want to send a parcel?
g   you want to catch a train?

Office du tourisme

HÔTEL

Garage

POSTE

PISCINE

Église

gare SNCF

8 You want to book a room in the Hôtel Royal in the summer. Look at
   the details below and work out what the missing information should
   say.

   a April   b a twin-bedded room
   c with bathroom   d for four nights
   e 28th June   f 2nd July
   g your name

   Cambridge, le 24 (a) ....

   Monsieur,

   Je voudrais réserver (b) ....

   ....

   (c) ....)

   (d) ....

   du (e) ....

   au (f) ....

   au nom de (g) ....
   Est-ce que vous pouvez confirmer la
   réservation, s'il vous plaît?

   Meilleures salutations,
   (g) ....

9 Can you complete the following grid?

Across
2 Vous habitez en ville ou à la ....?
5 C'est ....? Non, c'est à 200 mètres.
9 C'est pour six jours ou une ....?
11 Il y a un parking à .... de l'église.
12 Je suis secrétaire. Mon .... est en ville.
13 Vous .... anglais? (*speak*)
15 Ma chambre est au premier ....
16 Il y a .... magasins près d'ici?

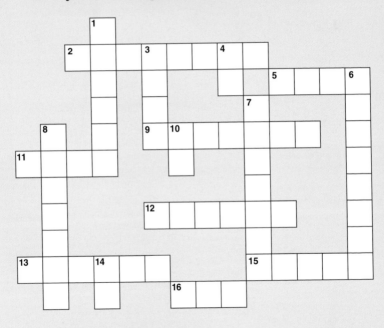

Down
1 Ma voiture est dans le ....
3 Prenez la première à droite, ... la deuxième à gauche.
4 Je .... travaille pas.
6 Octobre, ..., décembre.
7 Il habite dans un petit ....
8 Je suis infirmière à l' ....
10 Il y .... a deux.
14 Je voudrais une chambre pour .... 3 juin.

À quelle heure vous ouvrez?

understanding opening hours

... and making enquiries

enquiring about timetables

checking travel details

En France ...

although out of town shopping malls, superstores and shops in major urban areas are generally open all day Monday to Saturday, many other shops close at lunchtime then stay open until around 7 p.m. There are legal restrictions on Sunday opening, with most shops closed; many also close on Monday, except for **les boulangeries** *bakeries*.

Trains run seven days a week and you can travel in comfort between France's major cities in a TGV, **train à grande vitesse** *high-speed train*, the journey from Paris to Bordeaux takes just 3 hours. www.tgv.com has all the information.

Understanding opening hours

1   2•35 Listen to these key phrases.

À quelle heure vous ouvrez?   What time do you open?
On ouvre à sept heures.   We open at 7 o'clock.
... à huit heures.   ... at 8 o'clock.
À quelle heure vous fermez?   What time do you close?
On ferme à midi.   We close at 12 noon.

En français ...

on *one* is very often used to mean *we, you* or *they* when no-one in particular is meant. The verb which follows has the same ending as il/elle:

Ici on parle anglais.   *We speak English here./English spoken here.*

G5

---

2   2•36 Mélanie asks what time the baker's and the post office open tomorrow. Listen to the conversations and tick the right answers.

la boulangerie	6.00	8.00	9.00
la poste	7.00	8.00	9.00

En français ...

when talking about the time of day, the key word is **heure(s)**.
à trois heures   *at 3 o'clock*
à dix-neuf heures   *at 7 p.m./19.00 hours*
Minutes are simply added to these ...
à neuf heures quarante-cinq   *at 9.45*
à dix-neuf heures vingt   *at 7.20 p.m./19.20*

---

3   2•37 Listen to three shop assistants saying when the shop opens and match each assistant's answer with the right time, e.g. *1a*

a   09:30   b   08:30   c   14:15

... and making enquiries

4 **2•38** Listen to these key phrases.

C'est fermé aujourd'hui.	It's closed today.
C'est ouvert le dimanche?	Is it open on Sundays?
Quand ...?	When ...?
Le château est ouvert ...	The castle is open ...
... tous les jours ...	... every day ...
... sauf le lundi.	... except on Mondays.

lundi *Mon*	**vendredi** *Fri*
....	....
mardi *Tues*	**samedi** *Sat*
....	....
mercredi *Wed*	**dimanche** *Sun*
....	....
jeudi *Thurs*	
....	

5 **2•39** Mélanie now asks at the local grocer's whether they're open on Sundays. Listen and tick the right box. **Après-midi** means *afternoon* and **matin** means *morning*.

le dimanche matin:	ouvert ▢	fermé ▢
le dimanche après-midi:	ouvert ▢	fermé ▢

6 **2•40** She then enquires about opening hours for the castle and the museum. Listen and complete the details below.

	opening hours	day(s) closed
château		
musée		

Enquiring about timetables

1   2•41 Listen to these key phrases.

À quelle heure ...	At what time ...
... part le prochain train?	... does the next train leave?
... part le prochain car?	... does the next coach leave?
À quelle heure est-ce qu'il arrive?	At what time does it arrive?
Quand est-ce qu'il arrive?	When does it arrive?

2   2•42 Mélanie wants to visit Perpignan. Listen to her enquiring about train times and complete the details missing from the table.

	1	2	3
départ *departure*	14.25		15.45
arrivée *arrival*		15.25	

3   2•43 Now listen as she enquires about trains to the next village, Port-Vendres, famous for its fish market. Tick the right answer.

a   What is the best way for her to get there? (**En** means *by*.)

en car   **en train**   **en bus**

b   Where does the next coach leave from?

place du Marché	
place Saint-Jean	
rue du Marché	

c   What time does the next coach leave?

12.00   **12.15**   **12.30**

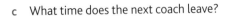

Checking travel details

1   **2•44** Listen to these key phrases.

un billet pour Paris	a ticket to Paris
un aller simple	a single
un aller-retour	a return
en première (classe)	first (class)
en seconde (classe)	second (class)
C'est quel quai?	Which platform is it?
Il faut changer à ...	You have to change at ...

2   **2•45** Listen to four snatches of conversation at the ticket office. Tick the correct details you hear.

a   single   return

b   first class   second class

c   platform 3   platform 7   platform 10

d   change at Nice   Marseille

En français ...

il faut means *it's necessary to, you have to* or *we have to*.

   Il faut réserver?   *Is it necessary to book?*

   Il faut aller à Nice.   *You have to go to Nice.*

---

3   Can you ask for the following tickets?

a   A single to Paris, second class.

b   Two returns to Nice, second class.

c   A single to Calais, first class.

put it all together

1 Match up the two halves of these sentences.

a	Je voudrais un aller	le prochain train?
b	Un aller-retour	pour Nice, s'il vous plaît.
c	À quelle heure part	à midi quinze.
d	Le train part	à Lyon.
e	Il faut changer	simple pour Paris.

2 Fill the gaps with the words from the list.

a Il faut .... à Marseille.
b Il .... réserver?
c Un aller- ...., s'il vous plaît.
d À quelle heure vous ....
   le dimanche?

faut
ouvrez
changer
retour

3 Read these signs: what do they mean?

a FERMÉ
LE MERCREDI

b OUVERT
TOUS LES JOURS
SAUF LE JEUDI

c ICI ON PARLE
ANGLAIS

4 Using **Il faut** .... ? how would you ask:

a if you have to book?
b if it's necessary to change in Paris?
c if you have to go to Port-Vendres?

now you're **talking!**

1   2•46 Imagine you're in a French railway station enquiring about timetables.

◆ Greet the lady at the desk and ask what time the next train for Boulogne leaves.
● **À 15 h 15.**
◆ Ask what time it arrives.
● **À 18 h 50.**
◆ Ask her to speak more slowly.
● **Oui. À 18 h 50.**
◆ Ask if you have to change.
● **Oui. Il faut changer à Paris.**
◆ Say you would like a single ticket, second class.
● **Voilà, monsieur.**
◆ Ask how much it is.
● **Ça fait 32,90 €.**
◆ Ask for the platform.
● **Quai six.**

2   2•47 You're at the baker's and enquire about opening hours.

◆ Greet the baker (a man).
● **Ah, bonjour.**
◆ Ask what time they open.
● **À 6 h 30.**
◆ Ask what time they close.
● **On ferme de 13 h à 15 h.**
◆ Ask whether it's open on Sundays.
● **Dimanche matin, oui, mais pas dimanche après-midi.**
◆ Say you don't understand and ask him to repeat.
● **Dimanche matin c'est ouvert, mais dimanche après-midi, c'est fermé.**

quiz

1 Does the sign **Fermé le dimanche** mean *Closed on Sundays* or *Closed on Mondays*?

2 If it was **midi**, what time would it be?

3 What might happen if you ignore the sign **Compostez votre billet**?

4 Is **un car** a coach, a car or a train?

5 How do you say *8 a.m.* in French?

6 What day comes after **mercredi**?

7 If you travel on the train **tous les jours**, do you travel every week or every day?

8 If you're told **Il faut payer un supplément**, what do you think you have to do?

9 How would you tell someone that the bank is open today?

10 And how would you tell them that the supermarket closes at 8 p.m.?

Now check whether you can ...

- ask about opening times and days
- ask when the next train, bus or coach leaves and arrives ...
  ... and understand the answer – using the 24-hour clock
- understand what day of the week something is available
- ask for a train ticket
- check essential travel details

You now know that a number of French and English words, such as **train**, **classe**, **changer**, are very much alike. But, as you have seen in this unit, you also have to look out for **faux amis** *false friends* which mislead you into thinking you know what they mean – **car** *coach*, **quai** *platform*, **composter** *to punch*. Look out too for **location**, which means *hire*.

Je voudrais du fromage, s'il vous plaît

buying food and drink

... and asking for more (or less)

saying how much you need

buying stamps and newspapers

En France ...

there are over 340 different cheeses. If you'd like to try lesser-known ones, look out for a **crémerie** or **fromagerie** *specialist cheese shop,* or head for the cheese stall at the market.

Ready-made dishes and salads to take away can be bought in a **charcuterie**, originally a specialist shop for ham, salami and other pork products.

You can buy stamps in most shops selling postcards or at a **bureau de tabac** *tobacconist's.* Supermarkets don't sell medicines. If you run out of aspirin, go to **la pharmacie** *the chemist's*, recognisable by a green cross.

Buying food and drink

1   2•48 Listen to these key phrases.

Je voudrais ...   I'd like ...
... du pain.   ... (some) bread.
... du fromage.   ... (some) cheese.
... de la viande.   ... (some) meat.
... des œufs.   ... (some) eggs.

2   2•49 Caroline is in the **magasin
d'alimentation** (general food shop). Listen
as she goes through her shopping list,
and tick off the items as you hear them
mentioned. Can you add the item she buys
that's missing from the list?

du pain bread
du beurre butter
de la confiture jam
du thé tea
du jambon ham
des œufs eggs
de la viande meat

En français ...

du, de la, de l' and des all mean *some*:

du pain   some bread
de la viande   some meat
de l'eau   some water
des œufs   some eggs

Although the word *some* is often left out in English e.g. *cheese
and wine*, it is always included in French – **du fromage et du vin**.

G3

3   2•50 Caroline is now at the **boulangerie**, buying some croissants.
Does she choose normal ones – **croissants nature** – or some with
extra butter – **croissants au beurre**?

4   How would you say you'd like some of the following:

● bread?   ● jam?   ● eggs?

... and asking for more (or less)

5 2•51 Listen to these key phrases.

Et avec ceci/ça?	Anything else?
Comme ça?	Like this?
Un peu plus.	A little bit more.
Un peu moins.	A little bit less.
Ce sera tout.	That will be all.

6 2•52 Caroline is in the **crémerie** buying two kinds of cheese –
roquefort and **gruyère**. Listen and link each of the assistant's
questions (on the left) with Caroline's replies (on the right).

a	Madame, vous désirez?	Du roquefort, s'il vous plaît.
b	Comme ça?	Un peu moins.
c	Voilà. Et avec ceci?	Ce sera tout, merci.
d	Comme ça?	Je voudrais du gruyère, s'il vous plaît.
e	Bien. Et avec ça?	Un peu plus, s'il vous plaît.

7 2•53 Listen to Paul buying some **brie**. In reply to **Comme ça?**, does
he ask for more or less? And what else does he buy?

8 How many French cheeses can you name in French? Look out for
them in your local supermarket. Make a list and practise asking for
them. You use **du** for all cheeses except those that start with a vowel
e.g. **de l'emmental**.

Saying how much you need

1   2•54 Listen to these key phrases.

Cent grammes.	100 grams.
Deux-cent-cinquante grammes de fraises.	250 grams of strawberries.
Une demi-livre de tomates.	Half a pound of tomatoes.
Une livre de champignons.	A pound of mushrooms.
Un kilo de pommes de terre.	A kilo of potatoes.

2   2•55 Caroline is at the **magasin de fruits et légumes** *greengrocer's.*
Number the items below in the order you hear her ask for them.

3   2•56 She then goes to the **magasin d'alimentation** for the following
items. Listen to find which quantity goes with which item. You'll need
to know **une tranche de** *a slice of* and **une boîte de** *a tin of.*

a	une boîte de ...	pâté
b	250 g de ...	jambon
c	une tranche de ...	pêches
d	quatre tranches de ...	gruyère
e	un kilo de ...	sardines

Buying stamps and newspapers

1 **2•57** Listen to these key phrases.

Vous vendez ...	Do you sell ...
... des journaux anglais?	... English newspapers?
... des cartes postales?	... postcards?
... des timbres pour l'Angleterre?	... stamps for England?
C'est joli.	It's nice/pretty.
C'est trop cher.	It's too expensive.
Je prends ...	I'll have ...

2 **2•58** Paul is at the **marchand de journaux** *newsagent's*. He has seen some German newspapers and wants to know whether they have English ones as well. They'll have some tomorrow, but when exactly?

3 **2•59** Now listen as he asks about a pen he has seen.

  a How much does it cost?
  b Can he afford it?

4 **2•60** Paul has chosen some rather expensive postcards. Listen as he buys some of them and some stamps.

How many postcards does he buy?	*a* 5	*b* 4	*c* 2
How much money does he spend?	*a* 2,12 €	*b* 2,82 €	*c* 2,92 €

En français ...

you use **à** when you want to say what price something is

un timbre à 70 centimes   *a 70-centime stamp*

---

put it all together

1   Béatrice is buying some salami. Read the dialogue and fill the gaps. **Celui-là** means *that one*.

Béatrice	**Bonjour, madame. Je .... du saucisson.**
Mme Chaillou	**Oui.**
Béatrice	**Quatre .... de celui-là.**
Mme Chaillou	**Quatre tranches de saucisson. Oui. Avec ...., madame?**
Béatrice	**Ce sera ...., merci.**

2   You need to buy a few things for a picnic. How would you ask for:

a   some bread?   b   250 grams of Brie?
c   a tin of pâté?   d   some butter?
e   three slices of ham? f   a kilo of tomatoes?
g   a kilo of bananas?   h   two bottles of mineral water?

3   Can you link these French shop signs to their English equivalents?

a	BOULANGERIE	newsagent's
b	MARCHAND DE JOURNAUX	general food shop
c	ALIMENTATION	cheese shop
d	FRUITS ET LÉGUMES	greengrocer's
e	CRÉMERIE	baker's

4   Unscramble the letters on the right to find items for sale in these shops.

a   **Crémerie**   magrofe
b   **Charcuterie**   nabjom
c   **Boulangerie**   oscrintas
d   **Fruits et légumes** momsep

now you're talking!

1. **2•61** Imagine you're at the grocer's.

- **Vous désirez?**
- ◆ Ask for a kilo of potatoes.
- **Oui. Avec ceci?**
- ◆ Half a pound of apples.
- **Voilà.**
- ◆ Ask if they sell ham.

- **Oui.**
- ◆ Say you'd like four slices.
- **Très bien. Et avec ça?**
- ◆ Ask for some Brie.
- **Oui. Comme ça?**
- ◆ Ask for a bit less.

- **Voilà.**
- ◆ Ask for six eggs and a tin of pâté.
- **Bien.**
- ◆ Say that's all and ask for the price.
- **Ça fait 8,50 €.**
- ◆ Give the money – say *There you are.*

2. **2•62** You're out buying postcards when you see a leather wallet.

- ◆ Say it's nice and ask how much it is.
- **36 €.**
- ◆ Say it's too expensive and that you'll have the postcards.
- **Alors, deux cartes postales.**
- ◆ Ask whether they sell stamps.
- **Oui. Alors deux cartes postales et deux timbres à 46 centimes.**
- ◆ Ask how much that is.
- **Ça fait 1,22 €.**

quiz

1 What can you buy in a **charcuterie**?
2 Would you buy a **camembert** in a **crémerie**?
3 If you're a vegetarian, which of the following can you eat:
   des pommes de terre, **du jambon**, **de la viande**?
4 How many **grammes** are there in **un kilo**?
5 What is a **saucisson**?
6 If something is **trop cher**, can you afford it?
7 Is **un peu moins** a bit more or a bit less?
8 If you want **des timbres**, would you go to a **pharmacie**?
9 What do you think is sold in **une chocolaterie, une animalerie, une fleuriste** and **un magasin de sports**?
10 If **un marchand de fruits** sells fruit, what's the French for *a wine merchant*?

Now check whether you can ...

- ask for common food items
- say how much you require
- ask for more or less
- buy stamps and newspapers
- recognise common shop signs

When learning a language, it can be very easy to underestimate how much you know. Go back occasionally to one of the very early units to prove to yourself how much French you've learnt. Think also about what you find easy ... and difficult. If you can identify your strengths and weaknesses, you can build on the strengths and find ways of compensating for the weaknesses.

Bon appétit!

enquiring about snacks

reading a menu

ordering a meal

saying what you like and don't like

En France ...

eating well is a priority and you'll have no trouble finding a restaurant to suit your taste and your budget. Many restaurants have short opening hours though, especially at lunch time. The most reliable time to have a meal is between 12 and 1.30 p.m. and between 7.30 and 9.30 p.m.

If you don't want a meal, most cafés, which tend to stay open all day, offer a range of snacks such as sandwiches, **croque-monsieur** *toasted cheese and ham sandwich* and **omelettes**. Traditionally the French love their meat, but don't despair if you're vegetarian. Vegetarianism is gaining in popularity and most places will offer **un plat végétarien** *vegetarian dish*.

Enquiring about snacks

1   2•63 Listen to these key phrases.

Qu'est-ce que c'est?	What is it?
C'est un croque-monsieur avec un œuf.	It's a toasted cheese and ham sandwich with an egg.
Qu'est-ce que vous avez comme sandwichs?	What do you have in the way of sandwiches?
Qu'est-ce que vous avez comme glaces?	What do you have in the way of ice creams?

2   2•64 Barbara is in a café and wants to know what a **croque-madame** is. Listen and tick the right answer.

> Qu'est-ce que c'est, un croque-madame?

a   a toasted cheese sandwich
b   a toasted cheese and ham sandwich
c   a toasted cheese and ham sandwich with an egg

3   2•65 Paul and his sons are in a **salon de thé** *teashop*. They order something to eat. Listen and tick the items that they order.

a   **un sandwich au saucisson**   b   **un sandwich au fromage**
c   **une glace à la vanille**   d   **une glace à la fraise**
e   **une glace au chocolat**   f   **un sandwich au jambon**
g   **une glace au citron**

En français ...

the main ingredient or flavour is usually preceded by:
au for a masculine noun:

    une glace au chocolat   *chocolate ice cream*

à la for a feminine noun:

    une glace à la vanille   *vanilla ice cream*

à l' before a vowel or h:

    un gâteau à l'orange   *orange cake*

Reading a menu

1 **2•66** Listen to these key phrases.

Vous avez choisi?	Have you chosen?
Vous prenez …?	Will you have …?
Je prends …	I'll have …
le menu à 15 €.	the set menu at 15 euros.
Comme entrées …	For starters …

2 **2•67** Fabien Degrave is taking his wife and a friend out to celebrate her birthday. Does she want a set menu or to eat **à la carte**?

> **En français …**
>
> **prendre** *to take/to have* is a key verb. Its endings don't follow a regular pattern like those on page 46 and have to be learnt. Look out in this unit for **je prends**, **tu prends** and **vous prenez**; you'll find the complete verb on page 123.

3 **2•68** Read the set menu they're given, then listen and tick the starters they order.

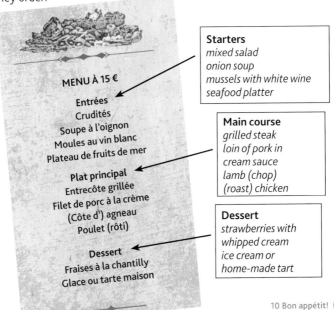

MENU À 15 €

Entrées
Crudités
Soupe à l'oignon
Moules au vin blanc
Plateau de fruits de mer

Plat principal
Entrecôte grillée
Filet de porc à la crème
(Côte d') agneau
Poulet (rôti)

Dessert
Fraises à la chantilly
Glace ou tarte maison

Starters
mixed salad
onion soup
mussels with white wine
seafood platter

Main course
grilled steak
loin of pork in
cream sauce
lamb (chop)
(roast) chicken

Dessert
strawberries with
whipped cream
ice cream or
home-made tart

Ordering a meal

1   2•69 Listen to these key phrases.

Comme plat principal?	For your main course?
Et comme légumes?	And for vegetables?
Et comme boisson?	And to drink?
Tout de suite!	Right away!
Bon appétit!	Enjoy your meal!

2   2•70 At the Restaurant Gourmet, the waitress asks the Degrave party how they like their meat done. Listen and tick the boxes.

	saignant *rare*	**à point** *medium*	**bien cuit** *well done*
Fabien			
Philippe			

3   2•71 She then asks for their vegetable order. Listen and tick their choices.

	haricots verts *beans*	**petits pois** *peas*	**frites** *chips*	**salade** *salad*
Thérèse				
Fabien				
Philippe				

4   2•72 What drinks do they order? Tick the right answer.

bourgogne   **bordeaux**   **côtes-du-rhône**
eau gazeuse *sparkling water*
eau non gazeuse *still water*
une carafe d'eau *jug of water*

5   2•73 Once the meal is over it's time to pay the bill – **l'addition**. Listen and find out whether they want any coffees first.

Saying what you like and don't like

1   **2•74** Listen to these key phrases.

J'aime ...	I like …
Je n'aime pas ...	I don't like …
C'est délicieux!	It's delicious!
C'est très bon!	It's very good!
Ce n'est pas bon!	It's not very nice!
La cuisine est excellente!	The cooking is excellent!

2   **2•75** Michel and Sabine are talking about the 15-euro menu. What do they like most? **Hors-d'œuvre** is another word for *starters*.

	Hors-d'œuvre	Plat principal
Sabine		
Michel		

En français ...

unlike in English, you use **le, la, les** when saying what you like and dislike:

J'aime la viande rouge.	*I like red meat.*
Je n'aime pas les fruits de mer.	*I don't like seafood.*

G3

3   **2•76** Now listen to three people describing what they like and don't like. Link each adjective on the left to the item on the right.

a	**délicieux**	**le bœuf bourguignon** *beef in red wine*
b	**très bon**	**le poulet rôti**
c	**excellent**	**le service**
d	**parfait** *perfect*	**le sorbet au cassis** *blackcurrant sorbet*
e	**excellente**	**le gâteau au chocolat**
f	**pas bon**	**la cuisine**

4   Now say in French what food and drink you like and don't like.

put it all together

1   Match up the two halves of the sentences.

a	Le poulet rôti	bien cuit, s'il vous plaît.
b	Je prends un steak	café, fraise ou cassis?
c	Qu'est-ce que vous avez	des haricots verts.
d	Qu'est-ce que c'est,	les fraises.
e	Je n'aime pas	le bœuf bourguignon?
f	Vanille, banane, chocolat,	est excellent!
g	Comme légumes, je prends	comme sandwichs?

2   Martine is enquiring about dessert.
Fill the gaps using the words in the list on
the right.

| prends |
| fraise |
| avez |
| comme |
| tarte |

Martine   Qu'est-ce que vous ....
comme glaces?
Serveur   Vanille, ..., chocolat ou café.
Martine   Et .... tartes?
Serveur   De la .... aux pommes.
Martine   Je .... de la tarte aux pommes.

3   If you were in Paris, what would you say to find out a café's
selection of the following?

a   sandwiches   b   omelettes   c   ice cream

4   Sort these words into the appropriate columns:

petits pois   fraises   moules   poulet   haricots verts
crudités   bœuf   pommes   soupe   agneau   champignons   glace

Entrées	Viandes	Légumes	Desserts

1   2•77 Imagine you're in a restaurant in Cannes with a
    French friend. You've already seen the menu when the waiter
    greets you.

- **Bonjour, vous avez choisi?**
- ◆ Say you'd like two 15 € menus.
- **Bien. Qu'est-ce que vous prenez comme entrées?**
- ◆ Ask for one pâté and one soup.
- **Et comme plat principal?**
- ◆ Ask what a **poulet basquaise** is.
- **C'est du poulet cuit dans une sauce tomate avec des
  poivrons** *peppers*.
- ◆ Order one chicken and one steak.
- **Steak saignant, à point ou bien cuit?**
- ◆ Ask for *medium*.
- **Bien. Et comme légumes?**
- ◆ Order some chips.
- **Et comme boisson?**
- ◆ Order a bottle of white wine and a bottle of sparkling
  mineral water.
- **Parfait.**

2   2•78 The starters have arrived.

- Tell your friend to enjoy his meal.
- ◆ **Merci. Toi aussi.**
- During the meal, you mention that the chicken is delicious.
- ◆ **Mon steak est excellent!**

A little later, the waiter asks about dessert.

- ◆ **Vous désirez du fromage ou un dessert?**
- Ask what they have in the way of ice cream.
- ◆ **Vanille, fraise ou café.**
- Order one coffee ice cream and one cheese.

Sometime later you call the waiter; ask for two coffees and
the bill.

quiz

1 Is an **hors-d'œuvre** a starter or a dessert?

2 What's the best time to have lunch in a French restaurant?

3 If the waiter says **Bon appétit!** does he want your order?

4 What is **l'addition**?

5 Is a **tarte aux fraises** an apple tart?

6 What's the difference between a **croque-monsieur** and a **croque-madame**?

7 What choice do you have if you see **Fromage ou dessert** on the menu?

8 Your meal is delicious. What would you say?

9 Fill in the missing words: **un gâteau** .... **citron; un sandwich** .... **poulet; une glace** .... **l'ananas.**

10 How do you ask what they have in the way of starters?

Now check whether you can ...

- order snacks and ice creams
- read a simple menu
- say what you want for starters, main course and dessert
- say how you want your meat cooked
- ask for the bill
- say what you like and don't like
- comment on the quality of the food

Bravo! Well done. You have completed **Talk French**.
And now prepare yourself for **Contrôle 3**, the final checkpoint which covers elements from the whole course, with some revision. Listen again to the conversations on the audio, test your knowledge of key phrases by covering up the English and use the quizzes and checklists on the final pages of each unit to assess how much you remember.

Contrôle 3

Imagine you have just arrived in France on holiday …

1   After a long drive, you stop at a café. You're feeling tired and you
    want to find out if there's a hotel nearby. Which of the following
    questions do you ask the waiter?

    a   **Où est l'hôtel de ville?**
    b   **Il y a un hôtel près d'ici?**
    c   **Où est l'hôtel?**

2   You also want to ask the waiter whether you can use the telephone.
    What do you say?

    a   **Vous voulez téléphoner?**
    b   **Il faut téléphoner?**
    c   **Je peux téléphoner?**

3   2•79 The waiter explains where the hotel is.
    Listen and make a note of the directions he
    gives you.

    C'est loin?

    ....

    ....

    How far away is it? ....

4   2•80 You finally arrive at your hotel and go to reception.

    a   How would you say you'd like a double room?

        ....

    Listen to the receptionist's reply.

    b   What type of room does she offer you?
    c   What is the number of your room?
    d   Which floor is it on?

5   At the hotel reception you pick up a restaurant card. Check any
    words you don't know in the glossary.

Restaurant
LA TAVERNE
15 € MENUS 20 €

Spécialités régionales
Poissons et viandes grillés
Salle climatisée et belle terrasse
Concert de flamenco le jeudi soir
Ouvert tous les jours sauf le lundi

a   What kind of food does this restaurant offer?
b   Would you go there on a very hot day? Why?
c   Which day would you go if you enjoy flamenco?
d   Which day is their closing day?

6   2•81 You decide to give the restaurant a try. You overhear the people
    at the next table ordering their meal. Listen and tick the correct
    options.

a   The woman wants her steak …
    ☐ rare
    ☐ medium
    ☐ well done

b   For vegetables, they choose …
    ☐ two portions of green beans
    ☐ one portion of green beans, one portion of chips
    ☐ one portion of chips

c   To drink, they order …
    ☐ red wine and sparkling mineral water
    ☐ white wine and still mineral water
    ☐ red wine and a jug of water

7   You fancy a boat trip, **une promenade en mer**. You see the following advertisement: read it through, then answer the questions below.

> ### Les transports maritimes
> ### ALBATROS
> **Renseignements et réservations**
> aux billetteries de Collioure de 10 h à 12 h et de 13 h 30 à 19 h.
>
> | | |
> |---|---|
> | **Promenade en mer:** | Toutes les heures (durée: 50 minutes) |
> | **Promenade de nuit:** | Avec musique et cocktail, tous les soirs, départ à 22 h. |

a   How often do the boat trips leave?
b   How long does the boat trip last?
c   When does the night boat leave?
d   When can you make a booking?

8   You decide to go on one of the boat trips and you shop for a picnic in the local village shop. You also need some stamps for your postcards home. How would you ask for the items pictured below?

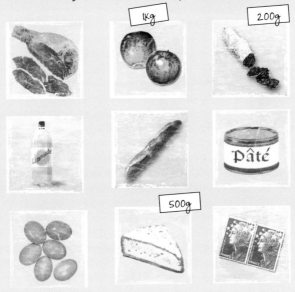

9   Later in the week, you decide to visit Paris for the day, but you don't want to drive there. At the railway station how would you ask …

   a   the time of the next train for Paris?
   b   what time it arrives?
   c   if it's necessary to change?
   d   for a return ticket?

10 During the train journey you strike up a conversation with the man sitting next to you, who comes from Switzerland. What would you tell him and what questions would you ask, using **vous**, to obtain the following replies?

   a   ………………………………
       Non, je suis suisse.

   b   ………………………………
       J'habite à la campagne.

   c   ………………………………
       Enchanté. Philippe Pasquier.

   d   ………………………………
       Non, je ne parle pas anglais.

   e   ………………………………
       Je suis architecte.

   f   ………………………………
       Non. Je suis divorcé.

   g   ………………………………
       Oui. J'ai une fille.

   h   ………………………………
       Elle a 14 ans.

   i   ………………………………
       Charlotte.

   2•82 Now he asks you some questions. Listen and be guided by the presenters on the audio.

Transcripts and answers

This section contains transcripts of all the conversations. Answers which consist of words and phrases from the conversations are given in bold type in the transcripts. Other answers are given separately, after each activity.

Unit 1

Pages 8 & 9 Saying hello and goodbye

2 ● Bonjour, **madame**.
  ◆ Bonjour, **Mademoiselle Canal**.
  ● Bonjour, monsieur.
  ◆ Ah, bonjour, **Madame Martinot**.

3 ● **Bonsoir**, Monsieur Faux.
  ◆ Bonsoir, madame.
  ● Bonsoir, mademoiselle.

4 ● **Salut**, Marc! Ça va?
  ◆ **Salut**, Julien! **Ça va**.

5 ● Bonjour, madame.
  ◆ Bonjour, monsieur.
  ● Salut, Luc.

7 ● Au revoir, **monsieur**.
  ◆ **Au revoir**, madame. Et merci!
  ● Au revoir, **madame**.
  ◆ Au revoir, madame. **Merci**!

8 ● Bonne nuit, **Pierre**!
  ◆ Bonne nuit, Julien!
  ● Bonne nuit, **Danièle**!
  ◆ Bonne nuit, Julien! Merci!

9 ● Bonjour, monsieur.
  ◆ Ça va?
  ● Merci, madame.
  ◆ Au revoir, mademoiselle.

Pages 10 & 11 Asking someone's name and introducing yourself

2 ● Comment vous appelez-vous? (1)
  ◆ François Suret. (2) Et vous? (3)
  ● Je m'appelle Camille Dupuis. (4)
  ◆ Enchanté. (5)

3 ● Comment tu t'appelles?
  ◆ Julie. Et toi, comment **tu t'appelles**?
  ● Je **m'appelle** Mélanie.

4 ● Vous êtes Mademoiselle Marty?
  ◆ Non.
  ● Oh, excusez-moi.
    Vous êtes Mademoiselle Marty?
  ◆ Non.
  ● Excusez-moi.

6 ● Mademoiselle Marty?
  ◆ Oui, je **m'appelle** Arlette Marty.
  ● Je **suis** Monsieur Bruno. Enchanté, **mademoiselle**.
  ◆ **Enchantée**, Monsieur Bruno.

Using the numbers 0 to 10

2 1 10 3 5 6

Page 12 Put it all together

1 a Merci; b Comment vous appelez-vous?; c Vous êtes ...?; d Je suis ...; e Bonsoir!; f Enchanté(e); g Ça va?; h Salut!

2 a Bonjour; b Bonsoir; c Salut; d Bonne nuit.

4 neuf; dix; six.

Page 13 Now you're talking!

1 ● Ah, bonjour, madame!
  ◆ **Vous êtes Madame Tubert?**
  ● Oui.
  ◆ **Bonjour, madame. Je suis ...**
  ● Enchantée.
  ◆ **Enchantée.**

2 ● Bonjour, madame!
  ◆ **Bonjour! Comment tu t'appelles?**
  ● Virginie. Et vous?
  ◆ **Je m'appelle ...**

3 ● Bonsoir, madame.
  ◆ **Bonsoir, monsieur, je suis ...**

- Enchanté. Pierre Larrot.
- **Enchantée.**

4 • **Au revoir, Madame Tubert, au revoir Virginie, et merci.**
 ◆ Au revoir …

Page 14 Quiz

1 To say hello, good morning or good afternoon; *2* tu; *3* Enchanté(e); *4* a good friend; *5* at night when going to bed; *6* Excusez-moi!; *7* Je suis …/ Je m'appelle …; *8* Comment tu t'appelles?; *9* Ça va (?).

Unit 2

Page 16 Giving your nationality

2 *a* Je suis français. (m)
 b Je suis anglaise. (f)
 c Je suis canadien. (m)
 d Je suis américain. (m)
 e Je suis anglais. (m)
 f Je suis australienne. (f)

3 l'Allemagne – allemand(e); l'Angleterre – anglais(e); le Canada – canadien(ne); l'Écosse – écossais(e); l'Espagne – espagnol(e); les États-Unis – américain(e); la France – français(e); l'Irlande – irlandais(e); le pays de Galles – gallois(e).

Page 17 Saying where you're from

2 • Je suis de **Stirling**, en **Écosse**.
 ◆ Je suis de **Madrid**, en **Espagne**.
 • Je suis de **Manchester**, en **Angleterre**.

3 • Marie-Pierre, vous êtes de Bayeux?
 ◆ Non, je suis de **Bordeaux**.
 • Et vous M. Michaud, vous êtes de Nantes?
 ◆ Non, je suis de **Nîmes**.

Page 18 Saying what you do for a living

2 • Quelle est votre profession?
 ◆ Je suis **architecte**.

- Et vous?
 ◆ Je suis **ingénieur**.
 • Et vous? Quelle est votre profession?
 ◆ Je suis **secrétaire**.

3 • Paul, quelle est votre profession?
 ◆ Je ne travaille pas. Je suis **retraité**.
 • Et vous, quelle est votre profession?
 ◆ Je suis **étudiant**.
 • Et vous, Marianne, vous êtes **étudiante**?
 ◆ Excusez-moi, je ne **comprends** pas.

Page 19 Using the numbers 11 to 20

2 *a* quatorze; *b* douze; *c* dix-neuf; *d* seize; *e* quinze.

3 **12 19 13 20 14 11 15**
 Seize (16) *was not mentioned.*

4 a **14**; *b* **16**; *c* **11**; *d* **13**

Page 20 Put it all together

1 • Vous êtes française?
 ◆ Non, non. Je suis anglaise.
 • Ah, vous êtes anglaise! Et vous êtes de Londres?
 ◆ Non, je suis de Chichester.

2 *a* Je suis de Sydney, en Australie. Je suis australienne.
 b Je suis de Manchester, en Angleterre. Je suis anglaise.
 c Je suis de Glasgow, en Écosse. Je suis écossais.
 d Je suis de Nice, en France. Je suis français.
 e Je suis de Los Angeles, aux États-Unis. Je suis américaine.
 f Je suis de Toronto, au Canada. Je suis canadienne.

3 France douze; Irlande quinze; pays de Galles onze; Angleterre quatorze; Canada dix-sept; États-Unis seize; Australie vingt; Allemagne dix-neuf.

4 *a* dix-neuf (19) *b* vingt (20) *c* treize (13) *d* quatorze (14)

Page 21 Now you're talking!

1 ● Excusez-moi, monsieur, la gare s'il vous plaît?
  ◆ **Je ne suis pas de Toulouse.**
  ● Vous n'êtes pas français?
  ◆ **Non, je suis anglais.**
  ● Vous êtes d'où?
  ◆ **Je suis de Birmingham. Vous êtes d'où?**
  ● Je suis de Séville.
  ◆ **Je ne comprends pas.**
  ● Je suis de Séville. Je suis espagnole.

2 ● Bonjour, madame. Vous êtes américaine?
  ◆ **Non, je suis ...**
  ● Vous êtes d'où?
  ◆ **Je suis de ...**
  ● Comment vous appelez-vous?
  ◆ **Je m'appelle ...**

3 ● Quelle est votre profession?
  ◆ **Je suis ingénieur. Quelle est votre profession?**
  ● Je suis professeur.

Page 22 Quiz

1 Je suis de Bristol; *2* a woman; *3* ne … pas *4* no; *5* fifteen; *6* the number of the department; *7* Je ne comprends pas; *8* américain; *9* italienne, égyptienne, marocaine; *10* avocat, caissier, pharmacien.

Unit 3

Pages 24 & 25 Introducing friends and family

2 ● Mon mari, Patrick.
  ◆ Ma femme, **Marion**, et mes amis, Émilie et Nicolas.
  ● Bonjour.

3 ● Voici **Benjamin**, mon mari. Il est **canadien**.
  ◆ Enchantée.
  ● Enchanté.

4 ● Vous êtes mariée?
  ◆ Je suis **divorcée**. Et vous?
  ● Je suis **célibataire**.

6 ● Isabelle, vous avez des enfants?
  ◆ Oui, j'ai **une fille**.
  ● Et vous, Émilie?
  ◆ **Non**, je n'ai pas d'enfants.
  ● Et vous, Marion, vous avez des enfants?
  ◆ Oui, j'ai trois enfants: **un fils** et **deux filles**.

7 Her daughter's name is Sabine, she does have a son (Luc) and she has one grandchild.

Page 26 Saying how old you are

2 21 vingt-et-un; 23 vingt-trois; 26 vingt-six; 30 trente; 38 trente-huit; 40 quarante; 45 quarante-cinq; 50 cinquante; 58 cinquante-huit; 60 soixante.

3 **25 33 40 42 58 67**

4 ● Tu as quel âge, Aurélien?
  ◆ J'ai **vingt-et-un** ans. (**21**)
  ● Et toi, Alex?
  ◆ J'ai **vingt** ans. (**20**)
  ● Et toi, Élisabeth?
  ◆ J'ai **seize** ans. (**16**)

5 ● Madame Blanc, vous avez quel âge?
  ◆ **Quarante-cinq** ans. (45)
  ● Vous avez quel âge, Monsieur Blanc?
  ◆ J'ai **cinquante-et-un** ans. (51)

Page 27 Talking about your family

2 ● Vous **avez** des enfants?
  ◆ Oui, j'ai une **fille**.
  ● Elle s'appelle comment?
  ◆ **Elle** s'appelle Valérie.
  ● Elle a quel **âge**?
  ◆ Elle **a** vingt-et-un **ans**.

3 ● J'ai 55 ans. J'ai deux enfants: Gérard, mon fils, a 28 ans et Isabelle, ma fille, a 32 ans.

- ◆ Je suis mariée et j'ai une fille.
- ● Je suis divorcée. J'ai deux enfants: mon fils a 15 ans et ma fille a 16 ans.

  a Sabine *b* Alain *c* Catherine

Page 28 Put it all together

1 *a* Chantal; *b* mon frère; *c* 13 ans;
d ma sœur; *e* Philippe; *f* ma femme.

2 *a* a; *b* avez; *c* ai; *d* as; *e* ai

3 *a* Je **m'appelle** Martine. *b* Mon **mari** s'appelle Marc. *c* J'ai un **fils** et une **fille**. Mon fils a **vingt-trois** ans. Il s'appelle **Benoît**. *e* Ma fille a **vingt-et-un ans**. Elle **s'appelle** Delphine.

Page 29 Now you're talking!

1 ● Bonjour, madame. Comment vous appelez-vous?
- ◆ **Sophie Smith. Bonjour.**
- ● Vous êtes mariée?
- ◆ **Oui, voici mon mari, Michael.**
- ● Vous avez des enfants?
- ◆ **Oui, j'ai un fils et une fille.**
- ● Et votre fille, elle s'appelle comment?
- ◆ **Elle s'appelle Anna.**
- ● Elle a quel âge?
- ◆ **Elle a douze ans.**
- ● Et votre fils, il s'appelle comment?
- ◆ **Il s'appelle Martin.**
- ● Il a quel âge?
- ◆ **Il a quatorze ans.**

2 ● **Vous êtes mariée?**
- ◆ Je suis divorcée.
- ● **Vous avez des enfants?**
- ◆ Oui, j'ai un fils, Théo.
- ● **Il a quel âge?**
- ◆ Il a quatorze ans. Ah, voici Théo!
- ● **Bonjour, Théo! Voici Martin et Anna.**

Page 30 Quiz

1 une fille; *2* mon; *3* célibataire;
4 Je n'ai pas d'enfants; *5* Elle a … ans;
6 Tu as quel âge?; *7* J'ai … ans; *8* 50.

Unit 4

Pages 32 & 33 Ordering a drink in a café

2 ● Vous désirez, monsieur-dame?
- ◆ Un thé, s'il vous plaît.
- ● Oui. Nature, lait, citron?
- ◆ **Un thé au lait**, s'il vous plaît.
- ● Oui. Et pour monsieur?
- ◆ Pour moi, **un thé au citron**, s'il vous plaît.
- ● Très bien.

3 ● Bonjour, messieurs dames. Vous désirez?
- ◆ **Une bière**, s'il vous plaît.
- ● **Un café**, s'il vous plaît.
- ◆ Pour moi, **une eau minérale**, s'il vous plaît. Et **un jus d'orange** pour Christine.
- ● Alors, une eau minérale, un café, une bière, et un jus d'orange.

4 *a* Alors, un coca, une limonade et **un thé au lait**.
b Un café, une pression et **un Schweppes**.
c Alors, deux bouteilles de champagne.
d Un vin **rouge** et une eau minérale.

5 ● Vous **désirez**?
- ◆ Deux cafés, un **grand** café et un **café** crème.
- ● Alors deux **cafés**, un **grand café** et un **café** crème.

Page 34 Offering, accepting or refusing a drink

2 ● Vous **voulez** un apéritif, Madame Blois?
- ◆ Non, merci. Pour moi, un verre d'eau.
- ● Et vous, Monsieur Blois? Un apéritif?
- ◆ Oui, **merci**.
- ● Qu'est-ce que vous **désirez**? Un martini, un porto, un whisky?
- ◆ Un porto, s'il vous plaît.

- D'accord. **Voilà**. À votre santé!
  Porto is port.

Page 35 Asking the price of drinks

2 70 soixante-dix; 73 soixante-treize;
79 soixante-dix-neuf; 80 quatre-vingts; 81 quatre-vingt-un; 92 quatre-vingt-douze; 94 quatre-vingt-quatorze; 100 cent

3 • Une bouteille de vin, alors ça fait **treize euros, quatre-vingt-cinq (13,85 €)**. Un verre de champagne, **sept euros, soixante-dix (7,70 €)**. Deux martinis, ça fait **neuf euros, quatre-vingts (9,80 €)**.

4 *a* Monsieur, s'il vous plaît, c'est combien?
Alors, un verre de champagne et un jus d'orange, ça fait **dix euros, quatre-vingts. (10,80 €)**
b Monsieur, s'il vous plaît, c'est combien?
Trois cocas, un Schweppes et un café crème, **douze euros, quatre-vingt-dix. (12,90 €)**
c Monsieur, s'il vous plaît, c'est combien?
Alors, deux bières, un verre de vin rouge et un café, ça fait **onze euros, soixante-quinze. (11,75 €)**

Page 36 Put it all together

1 *a* un café; *b* une bière; *c* un thé; *d* une limonade; *e* un coca; *f* un Orangina; *g* une eau minérale; *h* un jus de fruits.

2 *a* Qu'est-ce que vous désirez? Une limonade, s'il vous plaît.
b C'est combien? Ça fait douze euros.
c Vous désirez un thé au lait? Non, un thé au citron.
d Vous voulez un jus de fruits? Oui, un jus d'orange.
e Vous voulez un apéritif? Oui, un martini, s'il vous plaît.

3 • Vous désirez?
  ◆ Un thé, s'il vous plaît.

- Nature, lait, citron?
◆ Au lait.
- Voilà!
◆ C'est combien?
- Un euro, soixante.
◆ Voilà. Merci.

4 *a* cinquante-deux (52); *b* quatre-vingts (80); *c* soixante-treize (73); *d* quatre-vingt-dix (90).

Page 37 Now you're talking!

1 • **Monsieur, s'il vous plaît!**
◆ Bonjour, messieurs dames. Vous désirez?
- **Un grand café, un thé et un jus d'orange.**
◆ Très bien, merci.
- **Merci, monsieur. C'est combien?**
◆ Ça fait cinq euros, vingt.
- **Voilà.**

2 • Madame, monsieur, bonjour. Vous désirez?
◆ **Un coca et une bière.**
- Bouteille? Pression?
◆ **Pression, s'il vous plaît.**
- Très bien.
◆ **C'est combien?**
- Ça fait dix euros, soixante-dix.

3 • **Une bouteille de champagne, s'il vous plaît!**

4 • **Vous voulez un apéritif?**
◆ Oui, merci.
- **Qu'est-ce que vous désirez? Un martini ou un whisky?**
◆ Pour moi, un martini.
- Un whisky pour moi, s'il vous plaît.
◆ **Voilà. À votre santé!**

Page 38 Quiz

1 water – it's non-alcoholic; *2* un café crème; *3* café, coca, champagne; *4* 90; *5* pression; *6* À votre santé!; *7* The terrace, where you sit outside; *8* How much is it?; *9* Oui, merci; *10* un jus d'orange pour mon fils.

Contrôle 1

1 *a* À votre santé! *b* Bonne nuit!
   c Voilà! *d* Je ne comprends pas.
   e Enchanté! *f* Excusez-moi. *g* Ça va?

2 *1* Votre nom, s'il vous plaît?
   2 Madame Chevalier.
   3 Et votre prénom?
   4 **Christine**.
   5 Votre adresse, s'il vous plaît?
   6 **44** avenue de la Gare, 30100 Alès.
   7 Et votre numéro de téléphone?
   8 C'est le 04 **66** 98 35 **57**.

3 ● Je m'appelle Rosanna. Je suis
     espagnole et je suis de **Barcelone**.
   ◆ Je m'appelle Wilfried. Je suis
     allemand et je suis de **Berlin**.
   ● Je m'appelle Élisabeth. Je suis
     anglaise et je suis de **Brighton**.
   ◆ Je m'appelle Nicole. Je suis
     canadienne et je suis de **Toronto.**
   ● Je m'appelle Paul. Je suis **anglais**
     et je suis de **Newcastle**.

4 ● Vingt euros quarante-cinq.
   ● Sept euros, trente.
   ● Dix-sept euros, soixante-quinze.
   ● Quatorze euros, cinquante.
   ● Six euros, quatre-vingt-dix.
   ● Huit euros, soixante-quinze.
   (so number the prices 4, 2, 6, 1, 3, 5)

5 Paris, Calais, Arles, Tarbes, Nîmes,
   Cahors.

6 ● Bonjour. Vous désirez?
   ◆ **Un thé au lait, une bière et un
     verre d'eau, s'il vous plaît.**
   ● Très bien … La bière, pression ou
     bouteille?
   ◆ **Une bouteille, s'il vous plaît.**
   ● Vous êtes américaine?
   ◆ **Non, anglaise.**
   ● Vous êtes d'où?
   ◆ **Je suis de Bristol.**
   ● **C'est combien?**
   ◆ Ça fait 10,70 €.
   ● **Voilà. Merci.**

8 Dear Anna, My name is Julie. I am
   from Geneva, in Switzerland. I am
   14. I have a brother and a sister.
   My sister is 18, she is an au pair in
   Germany. My brother is 23. He is in
   France. He is married but he doesn't
   have any children. My father is an
   architect and my mother is a French
   teacher.

9 Café crème, jus de fruits, coca, vin
   rouge, bière, thé.

Unit 5

Pages 44 & 45 Asking where something is and how far it is

2 ● Où est le château, Virginie?
   ◆ C'est ici.
   ● Et le cinéma? Où est le cinéma?
   ◆ Le cinéma est en face de la gare.
   ● Où est le musée?
   ◆ Le musée est là.
   ● Et les magasins? Où sont les
     magasins, s'il vous plaît?
   ◆ Près de l'église.

4 ● Pardon, mademoiselle. C'est loin,
     la plage?
   ◆ Non, c'est à **10 minutes**.
   ● Excusez-moi, madame. **Le marché**
     … c'est loin?
   ◆ Non. C'est à **100 mètres**.
   ● Pardon, monsieur. C'est loin, **le
     centre-ville**?
   ◆ C'est à **cinq minutes**, monsieur.

5 *a* ● Où est **la poste**, s'il vous plaît?
       ◆ À côté du café, monsieur.
       ● Merci, madame.
   b ● Pardon, madame. Où est **l'hôtel**?
       ◆ L'hôtel est avant la gare,
         monsieur.
       ● Merci beaucoup.
   c ● Pardon, madame. Où est **le café**?
       ◆ En face de l'église, monsieur.
       ● Merci.
   d ● Pardon, monsieur. Où est **le
         musée**?

- ◆ Le musée est après le château, monsieur.
- ● Merci, monsieur.
- e ● Pardon, mademoiselle. Où est l'église?
- ◆ C'est à trois **cents** mètres de la banque.

Pages 46 & 47 Saying where you live and work

2 ● Vous habitez où?
- ◆ J'habite **dans un petit village**.
- ● Et vous, madame. Vous habitez où?
- ◆ Moi aussi, j'habite **à la campagne**.
- ● Vous habitez où, monsieur?
- ◆ J'habite **en ville**.
- ● Moi, aussi.

3 ● Bernard, tu habites où?
- ◆ J'habite **en ville**.

5 ● Mon frère travaille **chez Peugeot**.
- ◆ Ma sœur travaille pour **une compagnie américaine**. Elle travaille **à Paris**.
- ● Et ma femme travaille **dans un bureau**.
- ◆ Moi, je travaille chez moi.
  Bernard works at home.

6 a ● Je ne travaille pas. Je suis **au chômage**.
- b ● Je suis **étudiant**.
- c ● Je suis **mère de famille**.
- d ● Je ne travaille pas. Je suis **retraité**.

Page 48 Put it all together

1 a gare; b musée; c château; d marché.

2 Lille est à soixante-dix-sept kilomètres. Boulogne est à quatre-vingts kilomètres. Le Touquet est à quatre-vingt-quinze kilomètres. Montreuil est à quatre-vingt-dix-huit kilomètres.

3 a le; b l'; c la; d le; e le; f la

Page 49 Now you're talking!

1 ● Où est l'hôtel?
- ◆ C'est là.
- ● Où est le château?
- ◆ Le château, c'est là, en face de la mairie.
- ● C'est loin?
- ◆ Non, c'est à cinq minutes d'ici.
- ● Où sont le musée et l'église?
- ◆ Alors, le musée est ici et l'église est là.

2 ● Madame, s'il vous plaît. Un café au lait s'il vous plaît.
- ◆ Bien, madame.
- ● Où est la banque, s'il vous plaît?
- ◆ C'est là, à cent mètres du café.
- ● Vous habitez en ville?
- ◆ Non, j'habite dans un petit village à la campagne.
- ● C'est loin?
- ◆ Non, c'est à 20 kilomètres.

3 ● Vous êtes américaine?
- ◆ **Je suis + your nationality**
- ● Vous êtes d'où?
- ◆ **Je suis + where you're from**
- ● Vous habitez où?
- ◆ **J'habite + where you live**
- ● Quelle est votre profession?
- ◆ **Je suis + your profession**
- ● Vous travaillez où?
- ◆ **Je travaille + where you work**

Page 50 Quiz

1 the; 2 in an office; 3 après; 4 next to; 5 la gare; 6 quatre cents mètres; 7 C'est à dix minutes; 8 magasin; 9 Londres est à soixante-quinze kilomètres.

Unit 6

Pages 52 & 53 Asking for a specific place and making simple enquiries

2
a ● Pardon, monsieur. Il y a des taxis ici?

◆ Oui, madame, **place de la République**.

b ● Pardon, madame. Il y a un supermarché ici?

◆ Oui, **place du Marché**.

c ● Pardon, madame. Il y a une piscine ici?

◆ Oui, il y a une piscine **rue de la Gare**.

● Merci beaucoup, madame.

d ● Excusez-moi, mademoiselle. Il y a des magasins ici?

◆ Il y a des magasins **dans le centre-ville** à cinq cents mètres.

e ● Pardon, madame. Il y a un camping ici?

◆ Oui, **rue de Paris**, monsieur.

f ● Pardon, mademoiselle. Il y a un parking ici?

◆ Oui, **dans le centre-ville**.

3 ● Pardon, mademoiselle. Il y a un camping ici?

● Pardon, madame. Il y a une piscine ici?

● Pardon, monsieur. Il y a une poste ici?

● Pardon, monsieur. Il y a une banque ici?

5 ● Excusez-moi, monsieur. **Ma voiture est en panne.** Est-ce qu'il y a un garage près d'ici?

◆ À 12 km, madame.

● Oh, c'est loin! Il y a **une cabine téléphonique** près d'ici?

◆ Oui, il y en a une **là-bas**.

6

a ● Pardon, madame. Est-ce qu'il y a une poste près d'ici?

◆ Oui, monsieur. **En face de la banque.**

b ● Pardon, madame. Est-ce qu'il y a un supermarché près d'ici?

◆ Oui. **Là-bas, à côté de la banque**, madame.

c ● Excusez-moi, monsieur. Il y a une cabine téléphonique ici?

◆ Oui. **À côté de la poste**, madame.

● Merci, monsieur.

d ● Pardon, monsieur. Il y a un restaurant près d'ici?

◆ Il y a une pizzeria **en face du supermarché**.

The map is not correct. The pizzeria is opposite the supermarket.

Pages 54 & 55 Understanding basic directions and asking for help to understand

2

a ● Pardon, mademoiselle. Pour aller à l'office du tourisme?

◆ Prenez **la première à droite** et c'est là, **à gauche**. (**B**)

b ● Pardon, monsieur. Où est le marché, s'il vous plaît?

◆ Allez **tout droit** et prenez **la deuxième à gauche**. (**F**)

c ● Excusez-moi, monsieur. Où est l'hôpital, s'il vous plaît?

◆ Allez, allez **tout droit** et prenez **la troisième à droite**. (**D**)

3

a ● Pardon, monsieur. Où est la gare, s'il vous plaît?

◆ Allez **tout droit** et tournez **à droite après le pont**.

b ● Pardon, mademoiselle. Où est le cinéma, s'il vous plaît?

◆ Tournez **à gauche après le parking** et c'est **à gauche**.

c ● Excusez-moi, madame. Où est le camping, s'il vous plaît?

◆ Allez **tout droit** et tournez **à gauche après l'église et c'est à droite**.

All three places are correctly marked on the map.

5

● Pardon, Madame. Pour aller à l'Hôtel de Bordeaux?

◆ **Continuez tout droit. Prenez la troisième à droite et c'est à 200 mètres à gauche.**

● Oh. Vous pouvez parler plus lentement, s'il vous plaît?

- ◆ Continuez tout droit. Prenez la troisième à droite et c'est à 200 mètres à gauche.
- ● Merci beaucoup, madame.

- ◆ Pardon, monsieur. Le centre-ville, s'il vous plaît?
- ● **Tournez à droite et continuez tout droit. C'est à deux kilomètres.**
- ◆ Oh! … Vous pouvez répéter, s'il vous plaît?
- ● Alors, tournez à droite et continuez tout droit. C'est à deux kilomètres.

6 ● Il y a une **piscine** ici?
- ◆ Oui, place de la République. Prenez la **deuxième** à droite, puis tournez à **gauche**.
- ● Vous pouvez **répéter**, s'il vous plaît?
- ◆ Oui, **prenez** la deuxième à droite, puis tournez à gauche. C'est **place** de la République.
- ● Merci, madame.

7 ● Pardon, madame. Pour aller à la gare?
- ◆ Oui, alors **allez tout droit, prenez la troisième à gauche et c'est à deux cents mètres**.

8 ● Pardon, il y a une banque près d'ici?
- ◆ Il y a un camping près de la gare?
- ● Vous pouvez répéter, s'il vous plaît?

Page 56 Put it all together

1 pour; droit; tournez; deuxième; face; lentement

2 The swimming pool is next to the campsite, opposite **E**.

4 *a* eau; *b* droite; *c* infirmière; *d* garage; *e* banque; *f* autoroute

Page 57 Now you're talking!

1 ● **Pardon, madame, il y a un office du tourisme ici, s'il vous plaît?**
- ◆ Prenez la deuxième à droite et puis la première à gauche.

- ● **C'est loin?**
- ◆ Non, c'est à dix minutes.
- ● **Il y a une poste près d'ici?**
- ◆ Oui, il y en a une après la place du Marché, à gauche.
- ● **Vous pouvez répéter, s'il vous plaît?**
- ◆ La poste est après la place du Marché, à gauche.
- ● **Merci beaucoup et au revoir.**

2 ● **Il y a une banque près d'ici?**
- ◆ Oui, il y en a trois. Il y en a une place du Marché.
- ● **Vous pouvez parler plus lentement, s'il vous plaît?**
- ◆ Il y a une banque place du Marché. Continuez tout droit et prenez la deuxième rue à gauche.
- ● **C'est loin?**
- ◆ Oh non, c'est à cinq minutes.
- ● **Il y a un cinéma ici?**
- ◆ Non, il n'y a pas de cinéma ici.
- ● **Merci, au revoir, monsieur.**

3 ● Pardon. Il y a une banque près d'ici?
- ◆ **Il y a une banque là-bas, à droite.**
- ● Là-bas, à droite? C'est loin?
- ◆ **Non, c'est à deux minutes.**

Page 58 Quiz

1 il y a; *2* garage; *3* toll; *4* route départementale; *5* deuxième; *6* piscine; *7* en; *8* false: it means 'Could you speak more slowly?'; *9* il n'y a pas de marché.

Unit 7

Pages 60 & 61 Saying which type of room you want and how long you want it for

2 ● Bonsoir, madame.
- ◆ Oui monsieur, qu'est-ce que vous désirez?
- ● Je voudrais une chambre pour une personne.
- ◆ Avec douche ou salle de bains?

- **Avec salle de bains**, s'il vous plaît.

3 ● Bonsoir, monsieur.
  ◆ Bonsoir, madame. Je voudrais une chambre pour deux personnes.
  ● Oui. Une chambre avec deux lits ou avec un grand lit?
  ◆ **Un grand lit**, s'il vous plaît.
  ● Un grand lit.

4 a ● J'ai une chambre avec douche au deuxième étage ou une chambre avec salle de bains au troisième étage.
  ◆ Je prends la chambre avec salle de bains au **troisième étage**, s'il vous plaît. (3e)
  b ● J'ai une chambre avec salle de bains au premier étage ou une chambre avec douche au quatrième étage.
  ◆ Je prends la chambre **au premier étage**. (1er)

5 ● Je voudrais une chambre pour deux personnes avec douche.
  ● Je voudrais une chambre pour une personne avec douche et WC.
  ● Je voudrais une chambre avec deux lits, salle de bains et WC.

7 a Je voudrais une chambre pour deux personnes pour **trois nuits**, s'il vous plaît. (3 nights)
  b Je voudrais une chambre pour une personne pour **demain** seulement. (tomorrow only)
  c Je voudrais une chambre pour **ce soir**, s'il vous plaît. (tonight)
  d Je voudrais une chambre pour **une semaine**. (1 week)

9 ● Vous pouvez épeler votre nom, s'il vous plaît?
  ◆ BLANCHET.
  His surname is Blanchet.

Pages 62 & 63 Booking a room and paying for it

2 a Je voudrais réserver une chambre pour **le trois (3) avril**.

b Je voudrais réserver une chambre **du premier au quatre (1–4) juin**.

c Je voudrais réserver une chambre pour **le quatorze (14) juillet**.

d Je voudrais réserver une chambre **du douze au quinze (12–15) août**.

3 Je voudrais une chambre ... a pour le quinze juillet; b pour le dix avril; c pour le premier août; d du trois au six septembre; e du onze au quatorze mai; f du premier au quatre juin.

5/6
  ● Bonjour, monsieur.
  ◆ Bonjour, madame.
  ● Je voudrais une chambre, s'il vous plaît.
  ◆ C'est pour combien de personnes?
  ● Pour deux personnes, s'il vous plaît.
  ◆ Et pour combien de nuits?
  ● Pour trois nuits.
  ◆ Pour deux personnes, pour trois nuits ... avec salle de bains?
  ● Oui. C'est combien?
  ◆ **Cent quinze euros**, madame. (**115 €**)
  ● Le petit déjeuner est compris?
  ◆ Ah non. Le petit déjeuner est en supplément, **huit euros** par personne. (**8 €**)
  ● Je peux payer avec une carte de crédit?
  ◆ Oui, madame.

7 ● Je voudrais réserver une chambre pour deux personnes avec salle de bains pour une semaine.
  ● C'est combien?
  ● Le petit déjeuner est compris?
  ● Je peux payer avec une carte de crédit?

Page 64 Put it all together

1 a Je voudrais une chambre pour deux personnes.
  b Je voudrais une chambre avec deux lits.

c C'est pour une semaine.
d Je peux payer avec une carte de crédit?
e Le petit déjeuner est compris?
f C'est 8 euros en supplément.
g La chambre est au premier étage.
h Vous pouvez épeler, s'il vous plaît?

2 a Je voudrais une chambre pour deux personnes pour une semaine.
b Je voudrais une chambre pour une personne pour trois nuits.
c Le petit déjeuner est compris?
d Je voudrais une chambre au deuxième étage.

3 a yes – 6 €; b yes; c no; d no

Page 65 Now you're talking!

1 • **Bonjour, monsieur. Je voudrais une chambre pour ce soir.**
  ◆ Oui, madame. Qu'est-ce que vous désirez?
  • **Je voudrais une chambre pour deux personnes.**
  ◆ Très bien. Avec un grand lit ou avec deux lits?
  • **Avec deux lits.**
  ◆ Bien. Avec salle de bains ou avec douche?
  • **Avec salle de bains. C'est combien?**
  ◆ Une chambre pour deux personnes avec salle de bains, ça fait 60 euros.
  • **Le petit déjeuner est compris?**
  ◆ Non, il est en supplément.
  • **C'est combien?**
  ◆ Ça fait 6 euros 50 par personne.

2 • **Je voudrais réserver une chambre pour deux personnes avec deux lits et une douche pour le 22 juillet.**
  ◆ Oui, madame.
  • **Je peux payer avec une carte de crédit?**
  ◆ Oui, madame.
  • **C'est combien?**
  ◆ Ça fait 53 euros, madame.

Page 66 Quiz

1 No, it's the town hall; 2 when they are full; 3 a douche; 4 au quatrième étage; 5 janvier, juin and juillet; 6 DUPUIS; 7 true; 8 une semaine; 9 la chambre est pour ma fille; 10 il n'y a pas d'eau.

Contrôle 2

Pages 67–70

1 Prenez la direction **Bordeaux**. Juste après St Pey d'Armens, prenez la **troisième à droite**. Après cinq kilomètres, tournez **à gauche**. Continuez tout droit. Au village Saint-Sulpice, tournez **à droite**. Continuez pendant **500** mètres: la propriété est à droite **en face de** la rivière.

2 • Camille, vous habitez en ville ou à la campagne?
  ◆ J'habite au centre d'**un petit village** à la campagne, juste **à côté de la poste**.
  • Et vous travaillez où?
  ◆ Je travaille à Libourne, à 45 km.
  • Et vous travaillez dans une banque?
  ◆ Non, je travaille **dans un bureau. Je suis secrétaire**.
  • Vous avez quel âge?
  ◆ J'ai **trente-cinq ans**.

3 Alors, M. Rolland vient du **1ᵉʳ** au **5 mai**; M. Boulanger, du **27** au **30 juin**; Mme Aubert, du **13** au **15 juillet**; et Mlle Michaud, du **16** au **21 septembre**.

4 Avignon est à **72 km**, Marseille est à **85 km**, Cannes est à **93 km** et St-Tropez est à **78 km**.

5
a • Bonsoir, monsieur. Je voudrais réserver **une chambre avec salle de bains pour deux personnes**, s'il vous plaît. *(2 people with bath)*
b • Bonsoir, madame. Je voudrais réserver **une chambre avec**

douche. *(1 person, with shower)*

c   ● Bonjour, madame. Je voudrais
      réserver **deux chambres avec
      douche pour trois personnes**
      (3 people, 2 showers)

d   ● Bonjour, monsieur. Je voudrais
      réserver **une chambre pour une
      personne avec salle de bains.**
      (1 person, with bath)

6 *a* travaillez; travaille; *b* parles; parle
   c habitez; habite.

7 *a* GARAGE; *b* OFFICE DU TOURISME;
   c HÔTEL; *d* PISCINE; *e* ÉGLISE;
   f POSTE; *g* GARE SNCF.

8 *a* avril; *b* une chambre avec deux
   lits; *c* avec salle de bains; *d* pour
   quatre nuits; *e* 28 juin; *f* 2 juillet.

9 *Across*
   2 campagne; *5* loin; *9* semaine;
   11 côté; *12* bureau; *13* parlez;
   15 étage; *16* des
   Down
   1 garage; *3* puis; *4* ne; *6* novembre;
   7 village; *8* hôpital; *10* en; *14* le

Unit 8

Pages 72 & 73 Understanding opening hours and making enquiries

2 ● Pardon, madame. À quelle heure
      vous ouvrez demain?
   ◆ On ouvre **à 6 heures.**
   ● Pardon, monsieur. À quelle heure
      vous ouvrez?
   ◆ On ouvre la poste **à 9 heures,**
      madame.

3 *a* On ouvre à **neuf heures trente.**
   b On ouvre à **quatorze heures quinze.**
   c On ouvre à **huit heures trente.**

5 ● Pardon, monsieur, c'est ouvert le
      dimanche?
   ◆ **On ouvre le matin** de neuf heures
      à midi trente mais c'est **fermé
      l'après-midi.**

6 ● Pardon, monsieur, le château est
      ouvert le dimanche?
   ◆ Oui, oui. Le château est ouvert
      tous les jours de 9 h 30 à 19 h.
   ● Et le musée?
   ◆ Le musée est ouvert **de 10 h à midi
      et de 14 h à 18 h** tous les jours
      sauf le mardi.

Page 74 Enquiring about timetables

2 ● À quelle heure part le prochain
      train pour Perpignan?
   ◆ À 14 h 25, madame. Et il arrive à
      14 h 45.
   ● Et après?
   ◆ Il y a un train à **15 h 05.** Il arrive
      à 15 h 25. Puis il y a un train à
      15 h 45.
   ● À quelle heure est-ce qu'il arrive?
   ◆ À **16 h 06.**
   ● Merci, monsieur.

3 ● À quelle heure part le prochain
      train pour Port-Vendres?
   ◆ Il y a un train à midi trente mais
      la gare est loin. Il y a aussi **un car,
      place du Marché.** C'est juste là,
      en face.
   ● À quelle heure part le prochain
      car?
   ◆ **À midi.**
   ● Merci beaucoup, madame.

Page 75 Checking travel details

2

a ● Je voudrais **un aller-retour** pour
       Perpignan, s'il vous plaît.

b ● Un aller-retour **en première**, s'il
       vous plaît.

c ● C'est quel quai?
     ◆ **Quai numéro 7.**

d ● Il faut changer?
     ◆ Oui, il faut changer **à Marseille.**

3 *a* Je voudrais un aller simple en
       seconde/en deuxième classe pour
       Paris, s'il vous plaît.
   b Je voudrais deux aller-retour pour

Nice en seconde/en deuxième classe, s'il vous plaît.

c Je voudrais un aller simple pour Calais en première classe, s'il vous plaît.

Page 76 Put it all together

1 *a* Je voudrais un aller simple pour Paris; *b* Un aller-retour pour Nice, s'il vous plaît; *c* À quelle heure part le prochain train? *d* Le train part à midi quinze; *e* Il faut changer à Lyon.

2 *a* changer; *b* faut; *c* retour; *d* ouvrez

3 *a* closed on Wednesdays; *b* Open every day except Thursday; *c* English spoken here

4 *a* Il faut réserver?
b Il faut changer à Paris?
c Il faut aller à Port-Vendres?

Page 77 Now you're talking!

1 • **Bonjour, madame. À quelle heure part le prochain train pour Boulogne?**
 ◆ À 15 h 15.
 • **À quelle heure est-ce qu'il arrive?**
 ◆ À 18 h 50.
 • **Vous pouvez parler plus lentement, s'il vous plaît?**
 ◆ Oui. À 18 h 50.
 • **Il faut changer?**
 ◆ Oui. Il faut changer à Paris.
 • **Je voudrais un aller simple, en seconde.**
 ◆ Voilà, monsieur.
 • **C'est combien?**
 ◆ Ça fait 32,90 €.
 • **C'est quel quai?**
 ◆ Quai 6.

2 • **Bonjour, monsieur.**
 ◆ Ah, bonjour.
 • **À quelle heure vous ouvrez?**
 ◆ À 6 h 30.
 • **À quelle heure vous fermez?**

◆ On ferme de 13 h à 15 h.
 • **C'est ouvert le dimanche?**
 ◆ Dimanche matin, oui, mais pas dimanche après-midi.
 • **Je ne comprends pas. Vous pouvez répéter, s'il vous plaît?**
 ◆ Dimanche matin c'est ouvert, mais dimanche après-midi, c'est fermé.

Page 78 Quiz

1 closed on Sundays; 2 midday; 3 you might have to pay a fine; 4 a coach; 5 huit heures; 6 jeudi; 7 every day; 8 you have to pay extra; 9 la banque est ouverte aujourd'hui; 10 le supermarché ferme à vingt heures.

Unit 9

Pages 80 & 81 Buying food and drink and asking for more (or less)

2 • Alors, je voudrais du pain, de la confiture, du beurre, du thé, **du fromage**, du jambon, de la viande et des œufs.

3 • Je voudrais cinq croissants.
 ◆ Vous voulez des croissants au beurre ou nature?
 • **Au beurre**, s'il vous plaît.

4 • Je voudrais du pain, de la confiture et des œufs.

6 *a* • Madame, vous désirez?
 • Je voudrais du gruyère, s'il vous plaît.
 b • Comme ça?
 • Un peu plus, s'il vous plaît.
 c • Voilà. Et avec ceci?
 • Du roquefort, s'il vous plaît.
 d • Comme ça?
 • Un peu moins.
 e • Bien. Et avec ça?
 • Ce sera tout, merci.

7 • Je voudrais du brie, s'il vous plaît.
 ◆ Oui. Comme ça?
 • **Un peu plus**, s'il vous plaît.
 ◆ Et avec ça?

- Je voudrais **du gruyère**.
- Du gruyère … Comme ça?
- Très bien.
- Et avec ceci?
- Ce sera tout, merci.

8 For example: du brie, du camembert, du Boursin, du gruyère, etc.

Page 82 Saying how much you need

2 • Je voudrais 250 grammes de fraises, un kilo de pommes, une livre de champignons, une demi-livre de tomates, un kilo de bananes, trois livres de pêches et un kilo de pommes de terre, s'il vous plaît.

3 • Je voudrais **une boîte de sardines**.
- Voilà, madame. Et avec ceci?
- **250 grammes de gruyère**, s'il vous plaît.
- 250 grammes de gruyère …
- Je voudrais aussi **une tranche de pâté**.
- Comme ça?
- Très bien … Et **quatre tranches de jambon** et **un kilo de pêches**.
- Voilà, madame. Avec ceci?
- Ce sera tout, merci.

Page 83 Buying stamps and newspapers

2 • Pardon, madame. Vous vendez des journaux anglais?
- Des journaux anglais? **Demain matin**, monsieur.

3 • C'est joli! C'est combien?
- **28,85 €**, monsieur.
- Oh, c'est **trop cher**.

4 • Alors, je prends juste les cartes postales et … vous vendez des timbres?
- Oui. Des timbres pour l'Angleterre?
- Oui. Quatre timbres, s'il vous plaît. Ça fait combien?
- Alors quatre cartes postales à un euro et quatre timbres à quarante-six centimes, ça fait cinq euros

quatre-vingt-quatre, monsieur.
- C'est cher … euh … je prends juste deux cartes postales, alors.
- Très bien, monsieur. **Deux cartes postales** et deux timbres, ça fait **deux euros quatre-vingt-douze**. **(2,92 €)**

Page 84 Put it all together

1 • Bonjour, madame. Je **voudrais** du saucisson.
- Oui.
- Quatre **tranches** de celui-là.
- Quatre tranches de saucisson. Oui. Avec **ceci**, madame?
- Ce sera **tout**, merci.

2 Je voudrais … a du pain; b deux cent cinquante grammes de brie; c une boîte de pâté; d du beurre; e trois tranches de jambon; f un kilo de tomates; g un kilo de bananes; h deux bouteilles d'eau minérale.

3 a baker's; b newsagent's; c general food shop; d greengrocer's; e cheese shop

4 a fromage; b jambon; c croissant; d pommes

Page 85 Now you're talking!

1 • Vous désirez?
- **Je voudrais un kilo de pommes de terre.**
- Oui. Avec ceci?
- **Une demi-livre de pommes.**
- Voilà.
- **Vous vendez du jambon?**
- Oui.
- **Je voudrais quatre tranches de jambon, s'il vous plaît.**
- Très bien. Et avec ça?
- **Du brie, s'il vous plaît.**
- Oui. Comme ça?
- **Un peu moins.**
- Voilà.
- **Et six œufs et une boîte de pâté.**
- Bien.
- **Ce sera tout. C'est combien?**

- Ça fait 8,50 €.
- **Voilà.**

2 • **C'est joli! C'est combien s'il vous plaît?**
- 36 euros.
- **C'est trop cher. Je prends les cartes postales.**
- Alors, deux cartes postales.
- **Vous vendez des timbres?**
- Oui. Alors deux cartes postales et deux timbres à 46 centimes.
- C'est combien?
- Ça fait 1,22 €.

Page 86 Quiz

1 pork and delicatessen foods; *2* yes;
3 des pommes de terre (potatoes);
4 1000; *5* French salami sausage;
6 no – it's too expensive; *7* a bit less;
8 no, you'd go to **le tabac** or **la poste**;
9 chocolate, pets, flowers, sports gear;
10 un marchand de vin.

Unit 10

Page 88 Enquiring about snacks

2 • Qu'est-ce que c'est, un croque-madame?
- **C'est un croque-monsieur avec un œuf.**
- D'accord.
c is correct

3 • Qu'est-ce que vous avez comme sandwichs?
- Sandwichs au saucisson, au jambon …
- Vous avez des sandwichs au fromage?
- Ah, non, monsieur.
- Alors, **un sandwich au saucisson, un sandwich au jambon**, et qu'est-ce que vous avez comme glaces?
- Glaces à la vanille, au chocolat, à la fraise, au citron …
- Alors, **une glace à la vanille et une glace au chocolat**, s'il vous plaît.

- D'accord.

Page 89 Reading a menu

2 • Thérèse, tu prends un menu ou à la carte?
- **Je prends le menu à 15 euros.**
She wants the set menu.

3 • Messieurs dames, vous avez choisi?
- Oui, le menu à 15 euros.
- Bien. Qu'est-ce que vous prenez comme entrées?
- Moi, je prends **la soupe à l'oignon.** Et toi, Thérèse?
- **Les moules au vin blanc**, s'il vous plaît.
- Et moi, **les crudités.**

Page 90 Ordering a meal

2 • Et comme plat principal?
- Moi, je prends le filet de porc normande.
- Pour moi, une entrecôte.
- Bien cuit, saignant, à point?
- Alors, moi, **bien cuit**, s'il vous plaît. Et toi, Philippe?
- Pour moi, **saignant**, s'il vous plaît.

3 • Et comme légumes, haricots verts, petits pois ou frites?
- **Haricots verts**, s'il vous plaît. Et toi, Fabien?
- **Des frites**, s'il vous plaît.
- Pour moi **une salade**, s'il vous plaît.
- Entendu.

4 • Et comme boisson?
- Une bouteille de vin rouge …
- Du bordeaux, du bourgogne, un côtes-du-rhône?
- Du **bordeaux**, s'il vous plaît. Et une carafe d'eau?
- Non, non. Une bouteille d'**eau gazeuse**, s'il vous plaît.

5 • Vous prenez un café?
- **Oui, merci. Trois cafés** et l'addition, s'il vous plaît.
- Tout de suite, madame.

Page 91 Saying what you like and don't like

2 • Alors, Sabine, qu'est-ce que tu prends comme hors d'œuvre?
   ♦ Je n'aime pas les fruits de mer! Mais j'aime **la soupe à l'oignon**. Et toi?
   • Moi, j'aime **les moules**. Et comme plat principal, qu'est-ce que tu prends: entrecôte ou poulet?
   ♦ Je prends **l'entrecôte**: j'aime la viande rouge.
   • Moi, je n'aime pas la viande rouge: je prends **le poulet**.

3 • Hum … **le bœuf bourguignon** est **excellent**!
   ♦ Oui, c'est excellent!
   • Et **le service** est **parfait**!
   ♦ Oui, parfait!
   • Mais **le poulet rôti** n'est **pas bon**!
   ♦ **Le sorbet au cassis** est **très bon**. Et **le gâteau au chocolat**?
   • Hum … C'est **délicieux**! **La cuisine** est **excellente**.

4 For example: J'aime le poulet mais je n'aime pas les fruits de mer. J'aime les haricots verts et la salade. J'aime le vin rouge.

Page 92 Put it all together

1 a Le poulet rôti est excellent!; b Je prends un steak bien cuit, s'il vous plaît; c Qu'est-ce que vous avez comme sandwichs?; d Qu'est-ce que c'est, le bœuf bourguignon?; e Je n'aime pas les fraises; f Vanille, banane, chocolat, café, fraise ou cassis?; g Comme légumes, je prends des haricots verts.

2 avez; fraise; comme; tarte; prends

3 Qu'est-ce que vous avez comme …
   a sandwichs? b omelettes? c glaces?

4 *Entrées:* moules, soupe, crudités
   Viandes: poulet, bœuf, agneau
   Légumes: petits pois, haricots verts, champignons
   Desserts: glace, pommes, fraises

Page 93 Now you're talking!

1 • Bonjour … vous avez choisi?
   ♦ **Deux menus à 15 euros, s'il vous plaît.**
   • Bien. Qu'est-ce que vous prenez comme entrées?
   ♦ **Un pâté et une soupe.**
   • Et comme plat principal?
   ♦ **Qu'est-ce que c'est un poulet basquaise?**
   • C'est du poulet cuit dans une sauce tomate avec des poivrons.
   ♦ **Un poulet et un steak, s'il vous plaît.**
   • Steak saignant, à point ou bien cuit?
   ♦ **À point.**
   • Bien. Et comme légumes?
   ♦ **Des frites.**
   • Et comme boisson?
   ♦ **Une bouteille de vin blanc et une bouteille d'eau gazeuse.**
   • Parfait.

2 • **Bon appétit!**
   ♦ Merci. Toi aussi.
   • **Le poulet est délicieux!**
   ♦ Mon steak est excellent!
   • Vous désirez du fromage ou un dessert?
   ♦ **Qu'est-ce que vous avez comme glaces?**
   • Vanille, fraise ou café.
   ♦ **Une glace au café et un fromage.**
   • **Monsieur! Deux cafés et l'addition, s'il vous plaît.**

Page 94 Quiz

1 starter; 2 between 12 and 1.30; 3 no, he wants you to enjoy your meal; 4 the bill; 5 no, a strawberry tart; 6 a croque-madame is a croque-monsieur (cheese and ham toasted sandwich)

served with a fried egg; *7* cheese or a dessert; *8* C'est délicieux!; *9* un gâteau au citron; un sandwich au poulet; une glace à l'ananas; *10* Qu'est-ce que vous avez comme entrées?

Contrôle 3

1 b

2 c

3 • **Allez tout droit. Tournez à gauche et c'est la première rue à droite.**
   ◆ C'est loin?
   • Non, c'est à **500 mètres**.

4
a • Je voudrais une chambre pour deux personnes, s'il vous plaît.
   ◆ Il y a seulement **une chambre avec deux lits et avec douche**. C'est la chambre **221** au **deuxième étage**.
b A twin room with shower
c 221
d 2nd floor

5 *a* Local specialities, grilled fish and meat; *b* yes, it has air conditioning; *c* on Thursdays; *d* Monday.

6 • Et comme plat principal?
   ◆ Un steak avec **des haricots verts** pour moi.
   • Le steak saignant, à point ou bien cuit?
   ◆ **Saignant**, s'il vous plaît.
   • D'accord. Et pour monsieur?
   ◆ Une entrecôte grillée avec **des frites**.
   • Et comme boisson?
   ◆ **Une bouteille de vin rouge** … du bordeaux?
   • D'accord, et **une carafe d'eau**.◆   Très bien. Une bouteille de bordeaux rouge et une carafe d'eau.

a rare; b green beans and chips; c red wine and a jug of water

7 *a* every hour; *b* 50 minutes; *c* 10 p.m.; *d* 10–12 and 1.30–7 p.m.

8 Je voudrais … trois tranches de jambon; un kilo de pommes; deux-cents grammes de salami; une bouteille de limonade; du pain; une boîte de pâté; six œufs; une livre/cinq-cents grammes de fromage; deux timbres.

9 *a* À quelle heure part le prochain train pour Paris?
   b À quelle heure (est-ce qu') il arrive?
   c Il faut changer?
   d Je voudrais un aller-retour, s'il vous plaît.

10
a • **Vous êtes français?**
   ◆ Non, je suis suisse.
b • **Moi, je suis … Vous habitez où?**
   ◆ J'habite à la campagne.
c • **Je m'appelle …**
   ◆ Enchanté. Philippe Pasquier.
d • **Vous parlez anglais?**
   ◆ Non, je ne parle pas anglais.
e • **Je suis … Et vous?**
   ◆ Je suis architecte.
f • **Vous êtes marié?**
   ◆ Non. Je suis divorcé.
g • **Vous avez des enfants?**
   ◆ Oui. J'ai une fille.
h • **Elle a quel âge?**
   ◆ Elle a 14 ans.
i • **Elle s'appelle comment?**
   ◆ Charlotte.

   • Et vous, vous travaillez où?
   ◆ **Je travaille …**
   • Et vous habitez en ville?
   ◆ **J'habite …**
   • Vous êtes marié(e)?
   ◆ **Je suis …**
   • Vous avez des enfants?
   ◆ **J'ai … /Je n'ai pas d'enfants.**

grammar

Grammar explains how a language works. When you're learning a new language it really helps to learn some basic rules, which are easier to follow if you understand these essential grammatical terms.

Nouns are the words for living beings, things, places and abstract concepts: *daughter, vet, William, lion, hat, village, Bordeaux, measles, democracy*.

Articles are **definite**: *the* house, *the* houses, or **indefinite**: *a* house, *an* area, *some* houses.

Gender: in French every noun is either masculine (m) or feminine (f). This is its gender, and you need to know a noun's gender because words used with it, such as articles and adjectives, have alternative masculine and feminine forms.

Singular means one; **plural** means more than one.

Personal pronouns are words that take the place of a noun to avoid repeating it, e.g. *you, she, him, we, they, them*.

There are **informal** and **formal** versions of *you* in French: **tu** is informal, used with people you're very familiar with and call by their first name; **vous** is used with everyone else, particularly with someone older than you.

Adjectives are words that describe nouns and pronouns: *good idea*; *strong red wine*; *she's tall*; *it was weird*. In French, unlike English, they have alternative forms according to what they're describing.

Agreement: when a French article or adjective is used with a noun, it has to agree with, i.e. match, that noun in terms of whether it's masculine or feminine, singular or plural.

The **ending** of a word is its final letter(s). In English, a verb ending in *-ed* tells you it happened in the past. Endings are more varied in French, for adjectives as well as for verbs.

Verbs relate to doing and being, and are recognisable in English because you can put *to* in front of them: *to live, to be, to speak, to explore, to play, to think, to have, to need*. This is the **infinitive** of the verb, the form you find in the dictionary. French infinitives are identified by their ending, which can be **-er**, **-ir** or **-re**.

Regular verbs follow a predictable pattern, e.g. *I work, I worked, I have worked*; whereas **irregular** verbs are not predictable, e.g. *I eat, I ate, I have eaten*, and have to be learnt separately.

1 nouns

Every French noun is either masculine (m) or feminine (f). The nouns
for male people are masculine and females feminine: **le fils** *son*, **la mère**
mother, **le cousin** *male cousin*, **la cousine** *female cousin*, **le collègue** *male
colleague*, **la collègue** *female colleague;* but there's no foolproof means
of telling the gender of other nouns from their meaning, e.g. a train is
masculine (**le train**) while a car is feminine (**la voiture**).

So when you come across a new noun, make a point of learning a
masculine noun with **le** and a feminine noun with **la**. This is the only totally
reliable way of learning noun genders. The following endings are a useful
indication of gender, but watch out for the many exceptions.

masculine endings		feminine endings	
often ending in a consonant:	plus:	often ending in -e:	plus:
-c, -d, -g, -k, -s	-age	-ée, -ie	-ité
-non, -ron, -ton	-ège	-ance, -anse	-son
-et	-isme	-ence, -ense	-tion
-ment	-eau	-ière	
-ail	-ou	-ude, -ure	
-ier, -eur		-sse, -tte	
		-lle, -rre	

> Most of the time you'll be understood even if you use a wrong gender
> but a handful of nouns have different meanings depending on whether
> they're masculine or feminine, e.g. **le livre** *book,* **la livre** *pound;* **le tour**
> *tour/turn,* **la tour** *tower.*

2 plural nouns

As in English, most French nouns add **-s** in the plural: **un café** > **des cafés**;
un train > **des trains**. But nouns that end in:

- **-s**, **-x** or **-z** don't change: **un/des fils** *son, sons;* **une/des voix** *voice,
  voices;* **un/des nez** *nose, noses*
- **-eau** or **-eu** add **-x**, not **-s**: **un château** *castle* > **des châteaux**; **un jeu**
  game > **des jeux**. Plus a few ending in **-ou**: **un bijou** *jewel* > **des bijoux**
- **-al** and **-ail** change to **-aux**: **un animal** > **des animaux**; **un journal**
  newspaper, **des journaux**.

The added **-s** or **-x** is not pronounced.

Just as English has irregular plurals such as *man > men, child > children*, French also has a few exceptions, e.g. **un œil** *eye* > **des yeux** *eyes*; **Madame > Mesdames; Monsieur > Messieurs.**

G3 articles

In French, the words used for *the, a* and *some* depend on whether the following noun is masculine or feminine, singular or plural.

		the singular	*the* plural	*a/an*	*some*
m	*wine*	**le vin**	**les vins**	**un vin**	**des vins**
f	*town*	**la ville**	**les villes**	**une ville**	**des villes**

Le and **la** shorten to **l'** when the next word begins with a vowel or a silent **h**:

l'apéritif (m) *the aperitif*; **l'excellent vin** (m) *the excellent wine*; **l'hôtel** (m) *the hotel*

l'église (f) *the church*; **l'autre ville** (f) *the other town*; **l'huile** (f) *the oil*

French uses the definite article more than English does – most noticeably in generalisations such as **Je n'aime pas les champignons** *I don't like mushrooms* – but also before:

- countries: **la France, les États-Unis** *USA*
- abstract nouns: **C'est la vie.** *That's life.*
- languages: **le français, l'italien. Le, la** or **l'** is used with a language after **apprendre** *to learn* and **comprendre** *to understand*, but not after **parler** *to speak* or **en** *in*: **je comprends le français** but **je parle français, en français.**

French doesn't use **un/une** with nouns denoting occupation or religion: **Je suis médecin.** *I'm a doctor.* **Elle est musulmane.** *She's a Muslim.*

à, which can mean *at, in* or *to* combines with **le** and **les**:

| à + le → au | au cinéma |
| à + les → aux | aux États-Unis (m); aux îles Scilly (f) |

de *of, from,* also combines with **le** and **les**:

| de + le → du | de + les → des |

De + definite article can mean:

- *some*: **du vin, de l'eau et des olives** *some wine, water and olives.* In French, these are used even when English might leave them out.
- *of the*: **le parking du restaurant, le nom de la fille, la mère des enfants.** Some French expressions have **de** built in, e.g. **près de** *near*, **à côté de** *next to*: **près de l'église, à côté du restaurant.**

adjectives

An adjective is listed in a dictionary in the masculine singular, e.g. **important**, **français**, **ouvert**, **essentiel**, **nécessaire**, **rouge**. Unlike English, the ending of a French adjective varies according to whether the noun being described is masculine or feminine, singular or plural, i.e. noun and adjective have to agree/match.

For adjectives ending in a consonant or **é**, the feminine version adds **-e**, while in the plural both masculine and feminine add **-s**:

le garage est ouvert/fermé	**les garages sont ouverts/fermés**
la banque est ouverte/fermée	**les banques sont ouvertes/fermées**

If the masculine adjective ends in **-e**, the masculine and feminine versions are the same:

le vin est rouge	**les vins sont rouges**
la pomme est rouge	**les pommes sont rouges**

If the masculine adjective ends in **-s** or **-x**, the masculine singular and plural versions are the same:

le vin français	**les vins français**
la bière française	**les bières françaises**

Some adjective endings follow recognisable patterns:

	m/f		m/f
el	essentiel/essentielle	c	blanc/blanche; public/publique
en	italien/italienne	f	actif/active
er	premier/première	g	long/longue
et	complet/complète	x	délicieux/délicieuse

… and some common adjectives are very irregular: **beau/belle** *beautiful*; **doux/douce** *soft, gentle*; **faux/fausse** *fake, false*; **frais/fraîche** *fresh*; **nouveau/nouvelle** *new*; **vieux/vieille** *old*.

A French adjective generally goes after its noun when the two are together, e.g. **un voyage important**. Sometimes, for emphasis, it's put before the noun: **un important voyage** *a (truly) important journey*.

A few very common adjectives and numbers go before the noun: **beau** *beautiful*, **bon** *good*, **grand** *big*, **gros** *big/fat*, **jeune** *young*, **joli** *pretty*, **long** *long*, **mauvais** *bad*, **meilleur** *better/best*, **nouveau** *new*, **petit** *small*, **vieux** *old*, **vrai** *real*; **premier** *1st*, **second/deuxième** *2nd*, **troisième** *3rd*, etc.

Because of the different position of adjectives, French abbreviations can be the opposite of their English counterparts, e.g. the French for the *EU* is **UE** (**Union européenne**).

verbs

In a dictionary, a French verb is in its infinitive form, ending in **-er**, **-ir** or **-re**: e.g. **parler** *to speak,* **finir** *to finish,* **vendre** *to sell.* Removing the ending leaves you with the verb stem: **parl-**, **fin-**, **vend-**. Other endings can be added to this, according to who is carrying out the verb: *I speak* is **je parle** while *we speak* is **nous parlons**.

Each of the three verb groups has sets of endings, used for all regular verbs in that group. The following set indicates that the verb is happening at the present time: **je parle** translates *I speak, I'm speaking* and *I do speak*.

		parler	
je	*I*	parle	• Around 85% of French verbs end in **-er**, and they all use these endings except for **aller** *to go.*
tu	*you*	parles	
il/elle	*he/she it* m/f	parle	• The endings for **je**, **tu**, **il/elle** and **ils/elles** all sound identical
nous	*we*	parlons	• The **vous** ending sounds the same as the infinitive.
vous	*you*	parlez	
ils/elles	*they* m/f	parlent	

		finir	vendre	
je	*I*	finis	vends	• **je**, **tu** and **il/elle** endings sound the same.
tu	*you*	finis	vends	
il/elle	*he/she it* m/f	finit	vend	• The **ils/elles** ending of **-ir** verbs sound like *-eesse*.
nous	*we*	finissons	vendons	
vous	*you*	finissez	vendez	• In the **ils/elles** ending, the final consonant of the stem is sounded but not **-ent**.
ils/elles	*they* m/f	finissent	vendent	

Je shortens to **j'** before a vowel or an **h**: **j'aime**, **j'habite**.

There are two words for *you*, and the verb has a different ending depending on which one you're using:

tu: someone you call by their first name

vous: someone you don't know as well, older, or more than one person

On *one* is often used instead of *I, we, you* or *they* when it relates to no-one in particular. The verb used with **on** has the **il/elle** ending: **On peut payer avec la carte de crédit?** *Can I/we/one/you pay by credit card?*

Common **-er** verbs: **aider** *to help*, **aimer** *to like/love*, **chercher** *to look for*, **demander** *to ask*, **désirer** *to want*, **donner** *to give*, **écouter** *to listen*, **fermer** *to close*, **goûter** *to taste*, **habiter** *to live*, **jouer** *to play*, **laisser** *to leave*, **montrer** *to show*, **travailler** *to work*, **trouver** *to find*, **regarder** *to look at*, **tourner** *to turn*.

Some common **-ir** verbs drop the consonant before **-ir** and don't add **-iss** in the plural, e.g. **partir** *to leave*: **je pars**, **il part**, **ils partent**. A small number use **-er** endings, e.g. **ouvrir** *to open*: **elle ouvre**, **nous ouvrons**. Many **-ir** verbs are irregular.

The **-re** regular group is small; it includes **attendre** *to wait (for)*, **descendre** *to go/get down*, **entendre** *to hear*, **perdre** *to lose*, **répondre** *to answer*.

G6 asking questions

French questions don't use extra words like *do/does*. To change a statement into a question, you can

- raise the pitch of your voice at the end so that it sounds like a question;
- put **Est-ce que** (literally *Is it that*) in front of it;
- reverse the order of the subject and verb if the question is short and simple. However, this is less common:

Vous travaillez à Paris. *You work in Paris.*
Vous travaillez à Paris? *Do you work in Paris?*
Est-ce-que vous travaillez à Paris? *Do you work in Paris?*
Travaillez-vous à Paris? *Do you work in Paris?*

G7 negatives

Do and *does* are not used in negatives either. To say something negative, **ne** goes in front of the verb and **pas** after it.
Vous ne travaillez pas à Paris. *You don't work in Paris.*
Je n'aime pas les fruits de mer. *I don't like seafood.*

spelling changes

Some **-er** verbs with regular endings incur minor changes to the stem:

- in the **nous** ending, verbs ending in **-cer** change **c** to **ç** while verbs ending in **-ger** add **e**: **commencer** *to start* > **nous commençons**, **manger** *to eat* > **nous mangeons**.
- verbs ending in **-eler** double the **-l** except for **nous** and **vous**: **appeler** *to call* > **je m'appelle, comment vous appelez-vous?**;
- some verbs change or add an accent except for **nous** and **vous**: **répéter** *to repeat* > **je répète, nous répétons**; **acheter** *to buy* > **j'achète, nous achetons**.

key irregular verbs

	être *to be*	**avoir** *to have*
je / j'	**suis** *I am*	**ai** *I have*
tu	**es** *you are*	**as** *you have*
il/elle	**est** *he/she/it is*	**a** *he/she/it has*
nous	**sommes** *we are*	**avons** *we have*
vous	**êtes** *you are*	**avez** *you have*
ils/elles	**sont** *they are*	**ont** *they have*

	dire *to say*	**faire** *to do/make*
je	**dis** *I say*	**fais** *I do*
tu	**dis** *you say*	**fais** *you do*
il/elle	**dit** *he/she/it says*	**fait** *he/she/it does*
nous	**disons** *we say*	**faisons** *we do*
vous	**dites** *you say*	**faites** *you do*
ils/elles	**disent** *they say*	**font** *they do*

	aller *to go*	**venir** *to come*
je	**vais** *I go*	**viens** *I come*
tu	**vas** *you go*	**viens** *you come*
il/elle	**va** *he/she/it goes*	**vient** *he/she/it comes*
nous	**allons** *we go*	**venons** *we come*
vous	**allez** *you go*	**venez** *you come*
ils/elles	**vont** *they go*	**viennent** *they come*

	prendre *to take*	savoir *to know*	voir *to see*
je	**prends** *I take*	**sais** *I know*	**vois** *I see*
tu	**prends** *you take*	**sais** *you know*	**vois** *you see*
il/elle	**prend** *he/she/it takes*	**sait** *he/she/it knows*	**voit** *he/she/it sees*
nous	**prenons** *we take*	**savons** *we know*	**voyons** *we see*
vous	**prenez** *you take*	**savez** *you know*	**voyez** *you see*
ils/elles	**prennent** *they take*	**savent** *they know*	**voient** *they see*

	pouvoir *to be able to*	devoir *to have to*	vouloir *to want*
je	**peux** *I can/am able to*	**dois** *I have to/ must*	**veux** *I want*
tu	**peux** *you can*	**dois** *you must*	**veux** *you want*
il/elle	**peut** *he/she/it can*	**doit** *he/she/it must*	**veut** *he/she/it wants*
nous	**pouvons** *we can*	**devons** *we must*	**voulons** *we want*
vous	**pouvez** *you can*	**devez** *you must*	**voulez** *you want*
ils/elles	**peuvent** *they can*	**doivent** *they must*	**veulent** *they want*

Pouvoir, devoir and **vouloir** are known grammatically as **modal verbs**. The verb following them is used in the infinitive:

Je peux voir? *May I see?/Can I see?*
Elle peut rester si elle veut. *She can stay if she wants.*
On doit payer?/Nous devons payer? *Do we have to pay?*
Vous devez montrer les passeports. *You have to show your passports.*
Anton veut savoir. *Anton wants to know.*
Ils veulent manger. *They want to eat.*

Je voudrais *I would like* also comes from **vouloir**, but not from the present tense: **Je voudrais savoir** *I'd like to know*.

wordpower

Many hundreds of words are identical or very similar in English and French. However, they're the same only when written down: when they're spoken they sound quite different. Page 6 provides guidelines on the individual sounds of French, but a few French sounds don't exist in English and a few combinations of letters sound very different in the two languages. The following are the main aspects that can prove tricky for English speakers.

- Most final consonants are silent in French e.g. **ballet, restaurant**. This is particularly noticeable in plurals ending in **-s**, which sound the same as the singular. However, a final **c, f, l** or **r** is pronounced, e.g. **avec, chef, avril, au pair**, although there are exceptions.

- A final consonant is also sounded when followed by a word beginning with a vowel or most words beginning with **h**, for example the **vous** in **Vous habitez là-bas?** sounds like *vooz*.

- An accent on **e** changes the way it sounds (see page 6). Think **café crème**.

- A feminine adjective is generally formed by adding **-e** to the masculine, which can lead to a noticeable difference in the pronunciation. A silent consonant at the end of a masculine adjective is no longer silent, e.g. **petit/petite**, **anglais/anglaise**. And a nasal masculine ending is no longer nasal: **important/importante**.

- **ll** has two possible sounds. After most vowels it sounds like **l** in *ball*: **balle, elle, million, ville**; but it sounds like *y* in *yacht* when **-ill** follows a vowel, e.g. **bouteille, travailler**, and also in a few other words such as **fille**. Think **mille feuilles**.

- Unexpectedly, **oi** is pronounced *wah*: **moi, soir, croissant**.

- The French **r** is always rolled at the back of the throat.

- In English, the combination *tion* sounds like *shun*, whereas in French it sounds like *seeon*. Words like **education, national, emotion** sound very different in the two languages.

- The sound of the French **u** doesn't exist in English. To make this sound, position your lips to say *oo* but say *ee* instead without moving your lips. Try it with **du, tu** and **rue**.

- In French **y** is usually a vowel, sounding like *y* in *happy*: **lycée**; but it can also be a consonant, when it sounds like *y* in *yoga*: **yeux**.

nouns

Huge numbers of English and French nouns are identical in written form, for example nouns ending in **-acle, -age, -ble, -nce, -nt** and **-ion**: **miracle, page, table, distance, torrent, émotion, impression**.

Many more are almost identical:

🇬🇧	🇫🇷	
-ism	**-isme**	**altruisme, réalisme, sexisme**
-ist	**-iste**	**féministe, réaliste, touriste**
-ologist	**-ologue**	**cardiologue, gynécologue**
-or/our	**-eur**	**professeur, couleur, odeur**
-ty	**-té**	**beauté, université, humanité**
-y	**-ie**	**autonomie, technologie, industrie**

However, some French nouns do not mean what you might expect them to:

un car *coach*   *a car* **une voiture**
une cave *cellar*   *a cave* **une grotte**
la chair *flesh*   *a chair* **une chaise**
un chef is *a chief/head* as well as *a chef*
l'hôtel de ville is the *town hall*
une lime *a file* (tool)   *a lime* **un citron vert**
une prune *a plum*   *a prune* **un pruneau**
un préservatif *a condom*   *preservative* **le conservateur**
une pièce *a room/play/coin*   *a piece* **un morceau**
un stage *a training course*   *the stage* **la scène**
une veste *a jacket*   *a vest* **un maillot de corps**

Many English nouns are used routinely in French, e.g. **le weekend, le shopping, le match, le parking, le marketing**. In the field of technology, however, there's a drive to use French words, e.g. **l'ordinateur** *computer*, **la souris** *mouse*, **le clavier** *keyboard*, **le fichier** *file*, **le logiciel** *software*, **le matériel** *hardware*, **le mot de passe** *password*. You'll still hear English terms though: *an email* is **un courriel** but **un email** and **un mail** are widely used, as are **le web**, **un blogue** and **la wifi**.

adjectives

There are hundreds of English adjectives which you can convert to French if you know the endings to look out for.

-able, -ible:
possible, impossible, probable, improbable
La boîte n'est pas recyclable. *The box isn't recyclable*

-ent, -ant, adding **-e** in the feminine:
L'hôtel est excellent. *The hotel is excellent.*
Elle est très intéressante. *She's very interesting.*

-ic(al) → **-ique:**
Je suis allergique aux œufs. *I'm allergic to eggs.*
Ma fille est asthmatique. *My daughter is asthmatic.*

-ive → **-if**, with the feminine being **-ive:**
un passe-temps actif, **une vie active** *an active hobby/life*
Les prix sont excessifs. *The prices are excessive.*

-ous → **-eux (f -euse):**
Vous êtes très généreux. *You're very generous.*
La soupe est délicieuse. *The soup's delicious.*

Many adjectives ending in **-al** are the same in both languages but quite a few others change the **-al** for **-el** in French, **-elle** in the feminine:
le point central, la gare centrale *central point/station*
le parc industriel, la zone industrielle *industrial park/zone*
C'est phénoménal ... exceptionnel! *It's phenomenal ... exceptional!*

Not all adjectives mean what they appear to mean:

actuel *current*	*actual* **réel**
éventuel *possible*	*eventual* **ultime**
extra *superb*	*extra* **supplémentaire**
génial *brilliant*	*genial* **cordial, sympathique**
gentil *kind*	*gentle* **doux**
gros *fat*	*gross* **dégoûtant, brut** (financial)
large *wide*	*large* **grand**
misérable *destitute*	*miserable* **malheureux**
propre *clean/own*	*proper* **correct**
rude *harsh*	*rude* **impoli**
sympathique *nice, pleasant*	*sympathetic* **compatissant**

Just as many English adverbs add *-ly* to an adjective, many French ones add **-ment** to the feminine form: **généralement, immédiatement, probablement**.

verbs

Many French verbs are easy to recognise as they're so similar to their English equivalent. In many cases it's simply a case of adding **-er** or replacing the final letter(s) with **-er**. Some spelling adjustments are also required such as *c/ck* > **qu**.

🇬🇧	🇧🇪	
	-er	**bloquer, charmer, détester, skier**
-e	-er	**adorer, arriver, changer, réserver**
-ate	-er	**célébrer, éliminer, pénétrer, suffoquer**
-ise/ize	-iser	**maximiser, organiser, terroriser**
-ish	-ir	**abolir, démolir, finir, punir**
-ify	-ifier	**clarifier, identifier, justifier, vérifier**

Verbs that don't mean what they appear to mean include:

assister *to attend*	*to assist* **aider**
attendre *to wait for*	*to attend* **assister**
blesser *to wound*	*to bless* **bénir**
contrôler *to check*	*to control* **diriger, manipuler**
crier *to shout, scream*	*to cry* **pleurer**
draguer *to chat up*	*to drag* **traîner**
hâter *to hurry*	*to hate* **haïr**
passer *to sit* (exam)	*to pass* (exam) **réussir**
prétendre *to claim*	*to pretend* **faire semblant**
rater *to fail*	*to rate* **classer**
rester *to stay*	*to rest* **se reposer**
travailler *to work*	*to travel* **voyager**

In the field of technology, basic verbs include **améliorer** *to upgrade*, **effacer** *to delete*, **imprimer** *to print*, **installer** *to install*, **relancer** *to reboot*, **surfer (sur) l'internet** *to browse the internet*.

Scanner *to scan* is imported from English and used with French verb endings, e.g. **je scanne**, **vous scannez**.

Télécharger means *to download* as well as *to upload*, **uploader** is often used with French verb endings in order to differentiate between the two.

Test your knowledge with our online quiz at
www.bbcactivelanguages.com/FrenchGrammarQuiz

top ten essentials

1 Describing and commenting:
   C'est magnifique! *It's superb!*
   Ce n'est pas acceptable. *It isn't acceptable.*
   Il/Elle est très capable. *He/She is very capable.*

2 Talking about what's available:
   Il y a une piscine. *There's a pool.*
   Il y a des magasins. *There are shops.*
   Est-ce qu'il y a un café? *Is there a café?*
   Il n'y a pas de restaurant(s). *There is/are no restaurant(s).*

3 Talking about having:
   J'ai un vélo. *I've got a bike.*
   Tu n'as pas le plan? *Don't you have the map?*
   Nous avons des questions. *We have some queries.*

4 Asking what things are:
   Qu'est-ce que c'est? *What is it?*
   Comment dit-on … en français? *How do you say … in French?*

5 Asking where things are:
   Où est l'entrée/la sortie? *Where is the entrance/exit?*
   Où sont les autres? *Where are the others?*

6 Saying what you like:
   J'aime la France. *I like France.*
   J'aime voyager. *I like travelling.*

7 Saying you would like (to do) something:
   Je voudrais une réponse. *I'd like a reply.*
   Je voudrais répondre. *I'd like to reply.*

8 Saying/asking if you have to do something:
   Je dois aller chez mes parents. *I have to/must go to my parents'.*
   Nous devons partir. *We have to leave.*

9 Saying/asking if you can do something:
   Je peux attendre. *I can wait.*
   Je peux voir? *Can I see?*
   Nous pouvons revenir. *We can come back.*

10 Asking somebody to do something:
   Vous pouvez répéter s'il vous plaît? *Please could you say that again?*
   Vous pouvez parler (plus) lentement? *Could you speak (more) slowly?*
   … j'apprends le français. *I'm learning to speak French.*

French–English glossary

This glossary contains only those words and phrases, and their meanings, as they occur in **Talk French**. Parts of irregular verbs are given in the form in which they occur, usually followed by the infinitive in brackets.

A

à at; to; in; with
a (avoir) (he/she) has (to have)
l'abricot (m) apricot
l'accessoire (m) accessory
d'accord OK, agreed
actif active
actuel current
l'addition (f) bill
l'adresse (f) address
l'aérobic (f) aerobics
l'âge (m) age
l'agneau (m) lamb; la côte d'agneau lamb chop
ai (avoir) (I) have (to have)
aider to help
aimer to like; to love
l'alimentation (f) grocery shop
l'Allemagne (f) Germany
allemand German
aller to go
l'aller-retour (m) return ticket
l'aller simple (m) single ticket
allergique allergic
allez (aller) (you – formal sing and pl) go (to go)
alors then, so, well, now
améliorer to upgrade; to improve
américain American
l'ami (m) friend; boyfriend; partner
l'amie (f) friend; girlfriend; partner

l'an (m) year
l'ananas (m) pineapple
anglais English
l'Angleterre (f) England
l'animal (m) animal
l'animalerie (f) petshop
l'année (f) year
l'anniversaire (m) birthday; anniversary
août August
l'apéritif (m) aperitif
l'appartement (m) flat
m'appelle (s'appeler) (I) am called (to be called)
l'appétit (m) appetite; bon appétit enjoy your meal
apprendre to learn
après after, afterwards
l'après-midi (m/f) afternoon, in the afternoon
l'architecte architect (m/f)
l'arrivée (f) arrival
arriver to arrive
as (avoir) (you – informal) have (to have)
assez enough; rather
l'assiette (f) plate; platter
assister to attend
asthmatique asthmatic
attendre to wait (for)
au revoir goodbye
au / aux at/to/in the
aujourd'hui today
l'Australie (f) Australia
australien/ne Australian
l'autoroute (f) motorway
autre other

avant before
avec with
l'avenue (f) avenue
avez (avoir) (you – formal sing and pl) have (to have)
l'avocat/e lawyer (m/f)
avoir to have
avril April

B

la baguette French bread
la balle ball
la banane banana
la banque bank
beau beautiful (m)
beaucoup (de) much, many, a lot (of)
le beau-frère brother-in-law
le beau-père father-in-law
belle beautiful (f)
la belle-mère mother-in-law
la belle-sœur sister-in-law
le beurre butter; au beurre with butter
bien well
la bière beer
le bijou jewel
le billet ticket (train etc.)
la billetterie ticket service
blanc / blanche white
blesser to wound; blessé wounded
le bœuf beef
la boisson drink
la boîte box; container
bon/ne good

bonjour hello
bonne chance good luck
bonne nuit goodnight
bonsoir good evening
la boucherie butcher's shop
la boulangerie baker's shop
bourguignon from Burgundy
la bouteille bottle
le brie Brie (cheese)
le bureau office
le bureau de tabac tobacconist's
le bus bus; en bus by bus

C

c'est it is
c'est combien? how much is it?
ça that, it
ça va it's/I'm fine; OK
ça va? how are you?; how's it going?; all right?
la cabine téléphonique telephone box
le café coffee; café
le café crème white coffee
le/la caissier/ère cashier
le camembert Camembert (cheese)
la campagne country(side)
le camping campsite
le Canada Canada
canadien/ne Canadian
le car coach; en car by coach
la carafe jug, pitcher
la carotte carrot
la carte map, card, menu
la carte de crédit credit card
la carte postale postcard
le cassis blackcurrant
la catastrophe catastrophe

la cave cellar
ce this (m)
ceci this; avec ceci? anything else?
cela that
célébrer to celebrate
célibataire single
celui-là that one
cent hundred
le cent cent (100 = €1 euro)
le centre centre
le centre-ville the town/city centre
la cerise cherry
cette this (f)
la chair flesh
la chaise chair
la chambre bedroom, hotel room
la chambre d'hôte bed and breakfast
le champagne champagne
le changement change; le changement climatique climate change
changer to change
la charcuterie cold meats, pork butcher's
le chat cat
le château castle
chaud hot
le chef chief; chef
cher / chère dear, expensive; trop cher too expensive
chercher to look for
le cheval horse
chez at the home, company of
chez moi at home
le chocolat chocolate
la chocolaterie chocolate shop
choisir to choose
au chômage unemployed

le cinéma cinema
cinq five
cinquante fifty
cinquième fifth
le citron lemon
le citron vert lime
clarifier to clarify
la classe class; en première, seconde classe (in) first, second class
le clavier keyboard
le clic click; faire un clic droit/gauche right-/left-click
climatisé air-conditioned
le coca coke
le/la collègue colleague (m/f)
combien (de) how much, how many
comme like, as, in the way of
comme ça like that
commencer to start
comment how
comment tu t'appelles? what's your name? (informal)
comment vous appelez-vous? what's your name? (formal)
le commissariat police station
la compagnie company
complet/ète complete, full; nous sommes complets we're full up
composter to punch/stamp (ticket)
comprendre to understand; to include
comprends: je ne comprends pas I don't understand
compris included
le concert concert
confirmer to confirm
la confiture jam

continuer to continue, keep on
le contrôle checkpoint
contrôler to check
correct proper
la côte rib, chop
le côté side; **à côté de** next to
la côtelette cutlet
le courriel email
le/la cousin/e cousin (m/f)
le crédit credit
la crème cream
la crémerie cheese/dairy shop
la crêperie pancake shop
crier to shout; to scream
le croissant croissant
le croque-madame toasted ham and cheese sandwich with a fried egg
le croque-monsieur toasted ham and cheese sandwich
les crudités (f pl) raw vegetables
la cuisine cooking
cuit cooked; **bien cuit** well done (steak)

D

d' / de / du / de la / des of; from; some; any
dans in, into
la date date
décembre December
dégoûtant gross, disgusting
le déjeuner lunch
délicieux / délicieuse delicious
demain tomorrow
demander to ask
demi half
démolir to demolish
le/la dentiste dentist (m/f)
le départ departure

le département department (administrative area)
départemental departmental
descendre to go/get down
désirer to want; **vous désirez?** what would you like?
le dessert dessert
deux two
deuxième second
devoir to have to, must
différent different
dimanche Sunday; **le dimanche** on Sundays, every Sunday
dire to say
direct direct
le directeur manager, director
la direction direction
la distance distance
divorcé divorced
dix ten
dix-huit eighteen
dix-neuf nineteen
dix-sept seventeen
donc so, therefore
donner to give
la douche shower
doux / douce soft; gentle
douze twelve
draguer to chat up
droit right (-hand); **à droite** on, to the right; **tout droit** straight on
la durée duration

E

l'eau (f) water
l'eau gazeuse sparkling water
l'eau minérale mineral water
écossais Scots, Scottish
l'Écosse (f) Scotland

écouter to listen
l'éducation (f) education
effacer to delete
l'église (f) church
égyptien Egyptian
élégant elegant
éliminer to eliminate
elle she/it
elles they (f)
l'emmental (m) Emmenthal (cheese)
en in; of them
enchanté/e pleased to meet you (m/f)
encore yet, still
l'enfant (m/f) child
ensuite then, next
entendre to hear
entre between
l'entrecôte (f) steak; **entrecôte grillée** grilled steak
l'entrée (f) first course (of meal), starter; entrance
environ about, approximately
environnemental environmental
envoyer to send
épeler to spell
es (être) (you – informal) are (to be)
l'escalope (f) escalope (veal or pork fillet)
l'Espagne (f) Spain
espagnol Spanish
essentiel/le essential
est (être) (he/she) is (to be)
est-ce que lit. is it that; **est-ce qu'il y a ...?** is/are there ...?
et and
l'étage (m) storey, floor; **au premier étage** on the first floor
les États-Unis (m) United States
êtes (être) (you – formal

sing and pl) are (to be)
être to be
l'étudiant student
l'euro € (m) euro
éventuel/le possible
exactement exactly
excellent excellent
exceptionnel/le
exceptional
excessif / excessive
excessive
excuser to excuse
excusez-moi excuse me,
sorry
expliquer to explain
extra superb

F

face: en face (de)
opposite, facing you
faire to do; to make
fait: ça fait that comes
to
la famille family
fantastique fantastic
fatigué tired
il faut it is necessary,
you/we/one must
faux / fausse fake; false
la femme wife
fermé closed
fermer to close
février February
le fichier file
le filet de porc loin of
pork
la fille girl; daughter
le fils son
finir to finish; to stop
le/la fleuriste florist
(m/f); florist's shop
frais / fraîche fresh
la fraise strawberry
français French
le frère brother
les frites (f pl) chips
le fromage cheese
le fruit fruit
les fruits de mer (m pl)
seafood

G

gallois Welsh
le garage garage
la gare station
la gare SNCF railway
station
le gâteau cake
gauche left; à gauche
on/to the left
gazeuse sparkling; l'eau
gazeuse sparkling water
la gendarmerie police
station
généreux / généreuse
generous
génial brilliant
gentil/le kind
le gîte holiday house
la glace ice; ice cream
goûter to taste
le gramme gram
grand big, large
la Grande-Bretagne
Great Britain
la grand-mère
grandmother
le grand-père
grandfather
gravement seriously,
gravely
grillé grilled
griller to grill
gros / grosse fat; big
la grotte cave
le gruyère Gruyère
(cheese)

H

habiter to live
haïr to hate
le haricot bean
les haricots verts green
beans
l'heure (f) hour; time
l'hôpital (m) hospital
le hors-d'œuvre (m)
starter
l'hôtel (m) hotel
l'hôtel de ville (m) town

hall
huit eight

I

ici here; d'ici from here
identifier to identify
il he/it
il y a there is/are
ils they (m)
impoli rude
imprimer to print
l'infirmier/ère nurse
(m/f)
l'ingénieur engineer
(m/f)
inspirer to breathe in; to
inspire
installer to install
introduire to introduce
irlandais Irish
l'Irlande (f) Ireland
italien/ne Italian

J

j', je I
le jambon ham
janvier January
le jardin garden
le jeu game
jeudi Thursday; le jeudi
on Thursdays, every
Thursday
jeune young
joli pretty, nice
jouer to play
le jour day
le journal newspaper
joyeux / joyeuse happy;
joyeux anniversaire
happy birthday
juillet July
juin June
le jus juice; le jus de
fruits fruit juice
juste just, correct
justifier to justify

K

le kilo kilo
le kilomètre kilometre

L

l' / la / le / les the
là there
là-bas over there
laisser to leave
le lait milk
large wide
le légume vegetable
lentement slowly
la lime file (tool)
la limonade lemonade
le lit bed; un grand lit
a double bed; deux lits
twin beds
la livre pound (£ and lb)
le livre book
la location booking, hire
le logiciel software
loin far away; loin d'ici
far from here
Londres London
long/ue long
lundi Monday; le lundi
on Mondays, every
Monday

M

M. Mr
m' / me me, myself
ma my (f)
madame Mrs, Madam
mademoiselle Miss
le magasin shop
le magasin de fruits et
légumes greengrocer's
magnifique magnificent,
superb
mai May
maintenant now
la mairie town hall
mais but
la maison house
malheureux /
malheureuse miserable;
unhappy
manger to eat
le marchand seller
le marchand de
journaux newsagent's

le marché market
mardi Tuesday; le mardi
on Tuesdays, every
Tuesday
le mari husband
marié married
marocain Moroccan
mars March
le matériel materials;
hardware
maternel/le maternal
le matin morning; in the
morning
mauvais bad
le médecin doctor
meilleur better;
meilleures salutations
best wishes
le menu set menu
la mer sea
merci thank you
mercredi Wednesday; le
mercredi on Wednesdays,
every Wednesday
la mère mother
la mère de famille
housewife
mes my (pl)
les messieurs gentlemen
messieurs dames Ladies
and Gentlemen
le mètre (abb. m) metre
le métro underground
railway
midi midday, noon
mille thousand
minéral mineral; l'eau
minérale mineral water
minuit midnight
la minute minute
Mlle Miss
Mme Mrs
moi me, myself
moi aussi me too
moins less
le mois month
mon my (m)
monsieur Mr, Sir
montrer to show

le morceau piece
le mot word; mot de
passe password
la moule mussel
les moules au vin blanc
mussels in white wine
le muscle muscle
le musée museum
la musique music
musulman Muslim

N

nager to swim
national national
la nationalité nationality
nature plain
ne … pas not
ne … pas de no, not any
ne … plus no more, no
longer
nécessaire necessary
neuf nine
neuf / neuve new
le nez nose
le nom name, surname
non no
nous we
nouveau / nouvelle new
novembre November
la nuit night; at night

O

octobre October
l'œil (m) eye
l'œuf (m) egg
l'office du tourisme (m)
tourist office
l'omelette (f) omelette
on we/one/they
ont (avoir) (they) have
(to have)
onze eleven
l'orange (f) orange
l'ordinateur (m)
computer
organiser to organise
ou or
où where
oui yes
ouvert open

ouvrir to open

P

le pain bread
la panne breakdown; **en panne** broken down
par by; per
par personne per person
le parc park
pardon excuse me, pardon, sorry
les parents (m pl) parents; relatives
parfait perfect
parisien/ne Parisian
le parking car park
parler to speak
part (partir) (it) leaves (to leave)
partir to leave, to depart
pas not
pas de ... no ..., not any ...
passer to pass by; to sit exam
le passe-temps hobby
le pâté pâté
la pâtisserie pastry (cake); cake shop
payer to pay
le pays country
le pays de Galles Wales
le péage toll
la pêche peach
pendant for
pénétrer to penetrate
perdre to lose
le père father
la personne person
petit little, small
le petit déjeuner breakfast
les petits pois garden peas
un peu (de) a little (of)
un peu moins/plus a bit less/more
peux (pouvoir) (I) can (to be able)

la pharmacie chemist's
le/la pharmacien/ne pharmacist (m/f)
phénoménal phenomenal
la pièce room; play (theatre); coin
la piscine swimming pool
la place square (town)
la plage beach
plaire to please
plaît: s'il vous plaît please
le plan map
le plat dish
le plat principal main course (of meal)
le plateau platter
pleurer to cry
plus more; **un peu plus a** bit more
le point point; **à point** medium cooked steak
le poisson fish
poli polite
la pomme apple
la pomme de terre potato
le pont bridge
le porc pork
la porte door
le porto port
possible possible
la poste post office
le poulet chicken
pour for, (in order) to; **pour moi** for me
pouvez (pouvoir) (you – formal sing and pl) can (to be able)
pouvoir to be able to
précieux / précieuse precious
premier/ère first
prendre to take; to have (e.g. drink)
prends (prendre) (I) take (to take)

prenez (prendre) (you – formal sing and pl) take (to take)
le prénom first name
près near; **près de** near (to); **près d'ici** near here
présenter to introduce
le préservatif condom
la pression draught beer
prétendre to claim
principal main
privé private
le prix price; prize
prochain next
le professeur teacher
la profession job
la promenade trip; **la promenade en mer** boat trip
proposer to propose, to suggest
propre clean; own
la propriété house, property
provoquer to provoke; to cause
la prune plum
le pruneau prune
puis then
punir to punish

Q

qu', que that; than; what; which
qu'est-ce que ...? what ...?; **qu'est-ce que c'est?** what is it?
le quai railway platform
quand ...? when ...?
la quantité quantity
quarante forty
quatorze fourteen
quatre four
quatre-vingt-dix ninety
quatre-vingts eighty
quatrième fourth
quel / quelle what; what a ...; which?
la question question;

query

qui who, whom; which
quinze fifteen

R

rater to fail exam
réel actual; real
regarder to look at
la région region
régional regional
relancer to reboot
le(s) renseignement(s)
(m/pl) information
répéter to repeat
répondre to reply
la réponse reply
se reposer to rest
la réservation booking
réserver to reserve, to
book
les résidents residents
le restaurant restaurant
rester to stay
retraité retired
réussir to succeed
revenir to come back
la rivière river
le roquefort Roquefort
(cheese)
rôti roast
rouge red
la route road; **route**
départementale small
road; **route nationale**
main road
rude harsh
la rue street, road

S

sa his/her/its (f)
saignant rare (steak)
la salade salad, lettuce
la salle room, hall
la salle de bains
bathroom
le salon de thé teashop
salut! hi!; bye!
les salutations
greetings, wishes;
meilleures salutations
best wishes
samedi Saturday; **le**
samedi on Saturdays,
every Saturday
sans without
la santé health; **à votre**
santé! good health!,
cheers!
la sardine sardine
la sauce sauce
le saucisson French
salami
sauf except
savoir to know
la scène the stage
se himself/herself/itself/
themselves
second second; **en**
seconde (classe) (in)
second class
le/la secrétaire
secretary (m/f)
seize sixteen
la semaine week
semblant: faire
semblant to pretend
sept seven
septembre September
sera (être) (it) will be (to
be); **ce sera tout?** will
that be all?
sérieux / sérieuse
serious
le service service; service
charge
ses his/her/its (pl)
seulement only
si if
six six
la SNCF French National
Railways
la sœur sister
le soir evening; **ce soir**
this evening/tonight
soixante sixty
soixante-dix seventy
sommes (être) (we) are
(to be)
son his/her/its (m)

sont (être) (they) are
(to be)
le sorbet sorbet
la sortie exit
la soupe soup; **soupe à**
l'oignon onion soup
la souris mouse
la spécialité speciality
le stage training;
placement, internship
le steak steak
suffoquer to suffocate
suis (être) (I) am (to be)
suisse Swiss
la Suisse Switzerland
le supermarché
supermarket
le supplément extra
charge
supplémentaire extra
sur on
sûr sure; **bien sûr** of
course
surfer (sur) l'internet to
browse the internet
sympathique nice,
pleasant

T

ta your (f)
le tabac tobacconist's
la table table
la tarte tart; **tarte**
maison home-made tart
le taxi taxi
te you, yourself
(informal)
le téléphone telephone
téléphoner to telephone
la télévision television
terminer to finish
la terrasse terrace
tes your (pl)
le TGV (train à grande
vitesse) high-speed train
le thé tea
le timbre postage stamp
toi you, yourself
les toilettes (f) toilet

la tomate tomato
ton your (m)
toujours always, still
le tour tour; turn
la tour tower
tourner to turn
tous les jours every day
tout all, everything
tout de suite right away
toutes directions all directions
toutes les heures every hour
le train train
traîner to drag
la tranche slice
le transport transport
le transport maritime sea transport
le travail work, job
travailler to work
treize thirteen
trente thirty
très very
très bien very well, fine
trois three
troisième third
trop too
se trouver to be situated
trouver to find
tu you (informal)
typique typical

U
un / une a, an, one

V
va (aller) (it) goes (to go)
la vanille vanilla
varié varied, various
végétarien/ne vegetarian
le vélo bicycle
vendre to sell
vendredi Friday; le vendredi on Fridays, every Friday
venir to come
vérifier to verify
le verre glass
vert green
la veste jacket
veuf / veuve widowed
la viande meat
la viande rouge red meat
la vie life
vient (venir) (he/she) comes (to come)
vieux / vieille old
le village village
la ville town, city; en ville in (a) town
le vin wine

vingt twenty
la vitesse speed
voici here is/are; here you are
voilà there is/are; there you are
voir to see
la voiture car; carriage (train)
la voix voice
vos your (pl)
votre your
voudrais (vouloir) I'd like (to want, to wish)
vouloir to want, to wish; vous voulez ...? do you want ...?
vous you (formal)
voyager to travel
vrai real; true
vraiment really
la vue view

W
les WC (m pl) toilet, WC

Y
y there; il y a there is/are
les yeux (m pl) eyes

Z
zéro nought

English–French glossary

A

a/an un / une
able: to be able to pouvoir
to abolish abolir
about (approximately) environ
active actif/active
activity l'activité (f)
actual réel, vrai
address l'adresse (f)
to adore adorer
aerobics l'aérobic (f)
after; afterwards après
afternoon l'après-midi (m/f)
age l'âge (m)
air-conditioned climatisé
air conditioning la climatisation
all tout / toute / tous / toutes
all directions toutes directions
all right: all right?; how are you?; how's it going? ça va?
allergic allergique
altruism l'altruisme (m)
always toujours
American américain
and et
animal l'animal (m)
anything else? avec ceci?; autre chose?
aperitif l'apéritif (m)
appetite l'appétit (m)
apple la pomme
approximately environ
apricot l'abricot (m)
April avril
architect l'architecte (m/f)
arrival l'arrivée (f)
to arrive arriver

to ask demander
asthmatic asthmatique
at à; at the à l' / à la / au / aux
at home chez moi, à la maison
to attend assister à
August août
Australia l'Australie (f)
Australian australien/ne
avenue l'avenue (f)

B

bad mauvais
bakery la boulangerie
ball la balle
banana la banane
bank la banque
bathroom la salle de bains
to be être
to be able to pouvoir
to be called s'appeler
to be situated se trouver
beach la plage
bean le haricot
beautiful beau / belle
beauty la beauté
bed le lit
bed and breakfast la chambre d'hôte
bedroom la chambre
beef le bœuf; beef in red wine sauce bœuf bourguignon
beer la bière; draught beer la pression
before avant
best wishes meilleures salutations
better meilleur
between entre
bicycle le vélo
big grand
bike le vélo
bill l'addition (f)

biodiversity la biodiversité
birthday l'anniversaire (m)
bit: a bit (of) un peu (de); a bit more un peu plus; a bit less un peu moins
blackcurrant le cassis
to block bloquer
boat trip la promenade en bateau
to book réserver
book le livre
booking la réservation
bottle la bouteille
box la boîte
boyfriend l'ami (m), le petit ami, le copain
bread le pain
breakdown la panne
breakfast le petit déjeuner
bridge le pont
brilliant génial
broken down en panne
brother le frère
brother-in-law le beau-frère
to browse the internet surfer sur l'internet
bus le bus; by bus en bus
but mais
butcher's la boucherie
butter le beurre; with butter au beurre

C

café le café
cake le gâteau
campsite le camping
Canada le Canada
Canadian canadien/ne
capable capable
car la voiture
car park le parking

card la carte
cardiologist le/la cardiologue
carriage (train) la voiture
carrot la carotte
to carry on continuer
cashier le caissier / la caissière
castle le château
cat le chat
catastrophe la catastrophe
cave la grotte
to celebrate célébrer
cellar la cave
cent (100 = 1 euro) le centime, le cent
centre le centre
chair la chaise
champagne le champagne; a bottle of champagne une bouteille de champagne
to change changer
to chat up draguer
to check contrôler
checkpoint le (poste de) contrôle
cheers! à ta/votre santé!
cheese le fromage
chef le chef (de cuisine)
chemist's la pharmacie
cherry la cerise
chicken le poulet
chief le chef
child l'enfant (m/f)
chips (fries) les frites (f pl)
chocolate le chocolat; chocolate shop la chocolaterie
to choose choisir
chop: lamb chop la côte d'agneau
church l'église (f)
cinema le cinéma
city la ville; city centre le centre-ville

to clarify clarifier
class la classe; (in) first/second class en première/seconde classe
clean propre
to click cliquer
climate le climat; climate change le changement climatique
to close fermer; closed fermé
coach le car; by coach en car
coffee le café; white coffee le café crème; le café au lait
coin la pièce (de monnaie)
colleague le/la collègue
colour la couleur
to come venir
to come back revenir
company (business) la société, la compagnie
complete (full) complet / complète
computer l'ordinateur (m)
concert le concert
condom le préservatif
to confirm confirmer
container le récipient, la boîte
to continue continuer
cooked cuit
cooking: to do the cooking faire la cuisine
country le pays
country(side) la campagne
course (study) le cours; (dish) le plat
cousin le cousin / la cousine
cream la crème
credit le crédit
credit card la carte de crédit
to cry pleurer

current actuel/le
cutlet la côtelette; lamb cutlet la côtelette d'agneau

D
date la date
to date-stamp (ticket) composter
daughter la fille
day le jour; every day tous les jours
dear cher / chère
December décembre
to delete effacer
delicious délicieux / délicieuse
to demolish démolir
dentist le/la dentiste
department le département
departmental départemental
departure le départ
dessert le dessert
to detest détester
different différent
direct direct
direction la direction
director le directeur / la directrice
dish le plat
distance la distance
divorced divorcé
to do faire
doctor le médecin (m/f)
door la porte
double bed un grand lit, un lit deux personnes, un lit deux places
to download télécharger
to drag traîner
drink la boisson
duration la durée

E
to eat manger
egg l'œuf (m)
Egypt l'Égypte (f)
Egyptian égyptien/ne

eight **huit**
eighteen **dix-huit**
eighty **quatre-vingts**
elegant **élégant**
eleven **onze**
to eliminate **éliminer**
email **le courriel, l'email (m), le mél**
to end **terminer; finir**
engineer **l'ingénieur (m/f)**
England **l'Angleterre (f)**
English **anglais**
enjoy your meal **bon appétit**
enough **assez**
entrance **l'entrée (f)**
environmental **environnemental**
essential **essentiel**
evening **le soir**; this evening **ce soir**
everything **tout**
exactly **exactement**
excellent **excellent**
except **sauf**
exceptional **exceptionnel/le**
excessive **excessif / excessive**
to excuse **excuser**
excuse me **pardon; excusez-moi**
exit **la sortie**
expensive **cher / chère**; too expensive **trop cher**
to explain **expliquer**
extra **supplémentaire**; extra charge **le supplément**
eye **l'œil** (plural: **les yeux**)

F

to fail exam **rater**
fake **faux / fausse**
false **faux / fausse**
family **la famille**
fantastic **fantastique**

far **loin**; far from here **loin d'ici**
fat **gros**
father **le père**
father-in-law **le beau-père**
February **février**
feminist **féministe**
fifteen **quinze**
fifth **cinquième**
fifty **cinquante**
file (computer) **le fichier; le dossier**
to find **trouver**
fine **très bien; ça va**
to finish **finir; terminer**
first **premier / première**; on the 1st floor **au premier étage**
fish **le poisson**
five **cinq**
flat **l'appartement (m)**
flesh **la chair**
floor (storey) **l'étage (m)**
florist **le/la fleuriste**
for me **pour moi**
for, (in order) to **pour**
forty **quarante**
four **quatre**
fourteen **quatorze**
fourth **quatrième**
France **la France**
French **français**
fresh **frais / fraîche**
Friday **vendredi**; on Fridays, every Friday **le vendredi, tous les vendredis**
friend **l'ami (m) / l'amie (f)**
fruit **le fruit**; fruit juice **le jus de fruits**
full (no vacancies) **complet**

G

game **le jeu**
garage **le garage**
garden **le jardin**

generous **généreux / généreuse**
gentle **doux / douce**
gentlemen **les messieurs**
German **allemand**
Germany **l'Allemagne (f)**
to get off (bus/train) **descendre (de)**
to get on (bus/train) **monter (dans)**
girl **la fille**
girlfriend **l'amie (f), la petite amie, la copine, la petite copine**
to give **donner**
glass **le verre**
to go **aller**; to get to …? **pour aller à/au …?**
to go down **descendre**
good **bon/ne**; quite good **pas mal**
good evening **bonsoir**
good luck **bonne chance**
goodbye **au revoir**
goodnight **bonne nuit**
gram **le gramme**
grandfather **le grand-père**
grandmother **la grand-mère**
Great Britain **la Grande-Bretagne**
green **vert**
green beans **les haricots verts**
greengrocer's **le magasin de fruits et légumes**
greetings **les salutations**
to grill **griller**
grilled **grillé**; grilled steak **entrecôte grillée**
grocery shop **l'épicerie (f), l'alimentation (f)**
gross (disgusting) **dégoûtant**
gross (economy) **brut**
gynaecologist **le/la gynécologue**

H

half (noun) la moitié
half (adj) demi
hall (large room) la salle
hall (corridor) le couloir
ham le jambon
happy content; heureux
/ heureuse; joyeux /
joyeuse
happy birthday joyeux
anniversaire
hardware (IT) le matériel
(informatique)
harsh rude
to hate détester; haïr
to have avoir
to have to devoir
he il
health la santé
to hear entendre
hello salut, bonjour
to help aider
here ici; from here d'ici;
here is/are, here you are
voici/voilà
hi! salut!
hire la location
to hire louer
hobby le passe-temps
holiday cottage le gîte
home la maison; at my/
your home chez moi/
toi/vous
horse le cheval (m);
horses les chevaux
hospital l'hôpital (m)
hot chaud
hotel l'hôtel (m)
hotel room la chambre
(d'hôtel)
hour l'heure (f)
house la maison
housewife la femme
au foyer; la mère de
famille
how comment
how are you?
(comment) ça va?

how much is it? c'est
combien?
how much?, how many?
combien (de)?
hundred cent
to hurry (se) hâter; se
dépêcher
husband le mari

I

I j', je
ice; ice cream la glace
to identify identifier
if si
immediately
immédiatement, tout
de suite
important important
to improve améliorer
in dans; en
included compris
information le(s)
renseignement(s) (m/pl)
intelligent intelligent
internship le stage
to introduce présenter
Ireland l'Irlande (f)
Irish irlandais
is/are there …? est-ce
qu'il y a …?
it il / elle (subject
pronoun); le / la / l'
(object pronoun)
Italian italien
Italy l'Italie (f)

J

jacket la veste
jam la confiture
January janvier
jewel le bijou (pl: les
bijoux)
job la profession; le
travail
journalism le
journalisme
jug la carafe
juice le jus
July juillet

June juin
to justify justifier

K

keyboard le clavier
kilo le kilo
kilometre le kilomètre
kind gentil/le
to know (a fact) savoir;
(to be acquainted with)
connaître

L

Ladies and Gentlemen
messieurs dames
lamb l'agneau (m)
lamb cutlet la côtelette
d'agneau
large grand
lawyer l'avocat/e
to learn apprendre
to leave partir (a place);
laisser
left gauche; on/to the
left à gauche
lemon le citron
lemonade la limonade
less moins
lettuce la laitue, la
salade
life la vie
to like aimer; what
would you like? vous
désirez?
like (as) comme
like that comme ça
lime le citron vert
to listen écouter
little petit; a little (of)
un peu (de)
to live habiter; vivre
London Londres
long long/ue
to look at regarder
to look for chercher
to lose perdre
lot: a lot (of) beaucoup
(de)
to love aimer

lunch le déjeuner

M

magnificent magnifique
main course le plat principal
to make faire
manager le directeur / la directrice
many beaucoup (de)
map le plan; la carte
March mars
market le marché
married marié
maternal maternel / maternelle
May mai
me me; moi: me too moi aussi
meat la viande; red meat la viande rouge
medium cooked (steak) à point
menu la carte; le menu
metre le mètre (abb. m)
midday midi
midnight minuit
milk le lait
mineral minéral; mineral water l'eau minérale
minute la minute
miserable malheureux / malheureuse
Miss mademoiselle; Mlle
Monday lundi; on Mondays, every Monday le lundi, tous les lundis
month le mois
more plus
morning le matin
mother la mère
mother-in-law la belle-mère
motorway l'autoroute (f)
mouse la souris
Mr Monsieur; M.
Mrs Madame; Mme

much beaucoup (de)
muscle le muscle
museum le musée
music la musique
Muslim musulman
mussel la moule;
mussels in white wine les moules au vin blanc
must devoir: you must: il faut; vous devez/tu dois
my mon (m) / ma (f) / mes (pl)

N

name (first name) le prénom
name (surname) le nom (de famille)
name: what's your name? comment tu t'appelles?; comment vous appelez-vous?; quel est ton/votre nom?
national national
nationality la nationalité
near près; near (to) près de
near here près d'ici
necessary nécessaire; it is necessary to il est nécessaire de; il faut
new nouveau / nouvelle; neuf / neuve
newsagent's le marchand de journaux
newspaper le journal
next prochain
next to à côté de
nice joli (attractive); gentil/le, aimable, sympathique
night la nuit
nine neuf
nineteen dix-neuf
ninety quatre-vingt-dix
no non
no …, not any … pas de …
no more; no longer ne

… plus
noon midi
nose le nez
not ne … pas
not much peu
nought (zero) zéro
November novembre
now maintenant
nurse l'infirmier / l'infirmière

O

October octobre
of de
of course bien sûr
of the du / de la / de l' / des
office le bureau
OK OK, d'accord; ça va
old vieux / vieille
on sur
one un / une
onion soup soupe à l'oignon
only seulement
to open ouvrir
open ouvert
opposite en face (de)
or ou
orange l'orange (f)
to organise organiser
other autre
over there là-bas

P

pancake la crêpe
pardon pardon; excusez-moi
parents les parents (m pl)
park le parc
to pass by passer
password le mot de passe
patient patient
to pay payer
peach la pêche
peas les petits pois
to penetrate pénétrer

per person **par personne**
perfect **parfait**
person **la personne**
pet shop **l'animalerie** (f)
pharmacist **le/la pharmacien/ne**
pharmacy **la pharmacie**
phenomenal **phénoménal**
piece **le morceau**
pineapple **l'ananas** (m)
placement (study) **le stage**
plain (yoghurt) **(le yaourt) nature**
plate **l'assiette** (f)
to play **jouer**
play (on stage) **la pièce**
pleasant **agréable, sympathique**
please **s'il te/vous plaît**
to please **plaire**
pleased to meet you **enchanté**
plum **la prune**
point **le point**
police station **le commissariat; la gendarmerie**
polite **poli**
pork **le porc**; loin of pork **le filet de porc**
port (drink) **le porto**
possible **possible**
post office **la poste**
postage stamp **le timbre**
postcard **la carte postale**
potato **la pomme de terre**
pound (£; lb) **la livre**
precious **précieux / précieuse**
to pretend **faire semblant**
pretty **joli**
price **le prix**
to print **imprimer**

priority **la priorité**
private **privé**
prize **le prix**
proper **correct**
property **la propriété**
to propose **proposer**
protection **la protection**
prune **le pruneau**
to punch (date-stamp) **composter**
to punish **punir**

Q

quality **la qualité**
quantity **la quantité**
query **la question**
question **la question**
quite **assez**

R

racism **le racisme**
railway platform **le quai**
railway station **la gare (SNCF)**
rare (steak) **saignant**
real **vrai, réel/le**
realism **le réalisme**
really **vraiment, réellement**
to reboot **relancer**
recyclable **recyclable**
red **rouge**
region **la région**
regional **régional**
rental **la location**
to repeat **répéter**
reply **la réponse**
to reply **répondre**
to reserve **réserver**
resident **le résident**
to rest **se reposer**
restaurant **le restaurant**
retired **retraité**
return ticket **l'aller-retour** (m)
right **droit**; on/to the right **à droite**
river **la rivière**
road **la route, la rue;**

main road **la grande route, la route nationale**
roast **rôti**
room **la pièce; la chambre; la salle**
rude **impoli**

S

salad **la salade**
salami **le saucisson**
sandwich **le sandwich**
sardine **la sardine**
Saturday **samedi**; on Saturdays, every Saturday **le samedi, tous les samedis**
sauce **la sauce**
to say **dire**
to scan **scanner**
Scotland **l'Écosse** (f)
Scots, Scottish **écossais**
to scream **crier**
sea **la mer**
seafood **les fruits de mer** (m pl)
second **deuxième; second**
secretary **le/la secrétaire**
to see **voir**
to sell **vendre**
seller **le marchand**
to send **envoyer**
September **septembre**
serious **sérieux / sérieuse**
seriously **sérieusement, gravement**
service; service charge **le service**
service included **service compris**
seven **sept**
seventeen **dix-sept**
seventy **soixante-dix**
sexism **le sexisme**
she **elle**
shop **le magasin**

to shout crier
to show montrer
shower la douche
side le côté
single (unmarried)
célibataire
single ticket l'aller
simple (m)
sister la sœur
sister-in-law la belle-
sœur
to sit an exam passer un
examen
six six
sixteen seize
sixty soixante
slice la tranche
slowly lentement
small petit
smell l'odeur (f)
so donc
soft doux / douce
software le logiciel
some du / de la / de l'
/ des
son le fils
sorry pardon; excusez-
moi
so-so comme ci comme
ça
soup la soupe
Spain l'Espagne (f)
Spanish espagnol
sparkling water l'eau
gazeuse (f)
to speak parler
speciality la spécialité
to spell épeler
sport le sport
sporty sportif / sportive
square (town) la place
stage la scène
to start commencer
starter l'entrée (f); le
hors-d'œuvre (m)
station la gare
to stay rester
steak l'entrecôte (f); le

steak
still encore; toujours
storey l'étage (m)
straight away tout de
suite
straight on tout droit
strawberry la fraise
street la rue
student l'étudiant/e
to succeed réussir
to suffocate suffoquer
to suggest proposer
Sunday dimanche; on
Sundays, every Sunday
le dimanche, tous les
dimanches
superb extra;
magnifique; superbe
supermarket le
supermarché
sure sûr
to swim nager
swimming pool la
piscine
Swiss suisse
Switzerland la Suisse

T

table la table
to take prendre
tart la tarte
to taste goûter
taxi le taxi
tea le thé
teacher le professeur
(m/f)
telephone le téléphone
to telephone téléphoner
television la télévision
ten dix
terrace la terrasse
thank you merci
that cela
that (which) qu' / que
that one celui-là
that, it ça
the l' / la / le / les
then alors; ensuite; puis
there là; y

there is/there are il y a
therefore donc
they ils (m pl); elles (f pl)
third troisième
thirteen treize
thirty trente
this ce / cette; this (one)
ceci
thousand mille
three trois
Thursday jeudi; on
Thursdays, every
Thursday le jeudi, tous
les jeudis
ticket (train etc.) le
billet; ticket office la
billetterie
time le temps, l'heure
(f); at what time? à
quelle heure?; Do you
have the time? Vous
avez l'heure?
tin la boîte
tired fatigué
to à; to the à l' / à la /
au / aux
tobacconist's le tabac
today aujourd'hui
toilet, WC les toilettes (f
pl), les WC (m pl)
toll le péage
tomato la tomate
tomorrow demain
tonight ce soir
too trop
tour le tour, la visite
tourist office l'office de/
du tourisme
tower la tour
town la ville; in (a) town
en ville
town centre le centre-
ville
town hall l'hôtel de ville
(m); la mairie
train le train
train (high-speed) le TGV
(train à grande vitesse)

transport le transport
to travel voyager
tray le plateau
true vrai
Tuesday mardi; on Tuesdays, every Tuesday le mardi, tous les mardis
to turn tourner
twelve douze
twenty vingt
twin beds deux lits (m pl), les lits jumeaux
two deux
typical typique

U

underground railway le métro
to understand comprendre; I don't understand je ne comprends pas
unemployed au chômage
unhappy malheureux / malheureuse
United States les États-Unis (m)
unmarried célibataire
to upgrade améliorer
to upload télécharger, uploader

V

vanilla la vanille
varied; various varié
vegetable le légume
vegetables (raw) les crudités (f)
vegetarian végétarien/ne
to verify vérifier
very très

very well très bien
view la vue
village le village
voice la voix

W

to wait (for) attendre
Wales le pays de Galles
to want vouloir; désirer
water l'eau (f)
we nous
Wednesday mercredi; on Wednesdays, every Wednesday le mercredi, tous les mercredis
week la semaine
well bien
well done (steak) bien cuit
well done! bravo!
Welsh gallois
what ...? qu'est-ce que ...?
what is it? qu'est-ce que c'est?
when quand
where où
which que
which ...? quel/le ...?
white blanc / blanche
who; whom qui
wide large
widowed veuf / veuve
wife la femme
wine le vin
with avec
without sans
word le mot
to work travailler
work le travail
to wound blesser; wounded blessé

Y

year l'an (m); l'année (f)
yes oui
yet encore; not yet pas encore
you tu (informal singular); vous (formal singular and plural)
young jeune
your ta (f) / ton (m) / tes (pl) (informal); votre (m/f) / vos (pl) (formal)

Z

zero zéro